Using
Microsoft PowerPoint

2023 Edition

Kevin Wilson

www.elluminetpress.com

Using Microsoft PowerPoint - 2023 Edition

Publisher: Elluminet Press
Director: Kevin Wilson
Lead Editor: Steven Ashmore
Technical Reviewer: Mike Taylor, Robert Ashcroft
Copy Editors: Joanne Taylor, James Marsh
Proof Reader: Mike Taylor
Indexer: James Marsh
Cover Designer: Kevin Wilson

eBook versions and licenses are also available for most titles. Any source code or other supplementary materials referenced by the author in this text is available to readers at

www.elluminetpress.com/resources

For detailed information about how to locate your book's resources, go to

www.elluminetpress.com/resources

Table of Contents

About the Author

With over 20 years' experience in the computer industry, Kevin Wilson has made a career out of technology and showing others how to use it. After earning a master's degree in computer science, software engineering, and multimedia systems, Kevin has held various positions in the IT industry including graphic & web design, digital film & photography, programming & software engineering, developing & managing corporate networks, building computer systems, and IT support.

He serves as senior writer and director at Elluminet Press Ltd, he periodically teaches computer science at college, and works as an IT trainer in England while researching for his PhD. His books have become a valuable resource among the students in England, South Africa, Canada, and in the United States.

Kevin's motto is clear: "If you can't explain something simply, then you haven't understood it well enough." To that end, he wrote the Exploring Tech Computing series, in which he breaks down complex technological subjects into smaller, easy-to-follow steps that students and ordinary computer users can put into practice.

Microsoft PowerPoint

PowerPoint is a widely used presentation application and is part of the Microsoft Office & Microsoft 365 suite. Originally developed by Forethought Inc, PowerPoint was initially released for the Macintosh in 1987. Microsoft acquired it shortly after its debut, launching it for Windows in 1990.

Over the years, PowerPoint has become essential for business, educational, and personal presentations, offering a wide range of features to create professional-looking slides.

PowerPoint allows you to combine text, graphics, multimedia elements, and animations to convey information effectively.

Before we begin, throughout this book, we will be using the resource files.

You can download these files from

elluminetpress.com/ppt

The software is designed to accommodate users of all skill levels, from beginners to advanced professionals, offering a user-friendly interface with drag-and-drop functionality, templates, and theme options that simplify the process of creating visually appealing presentations.

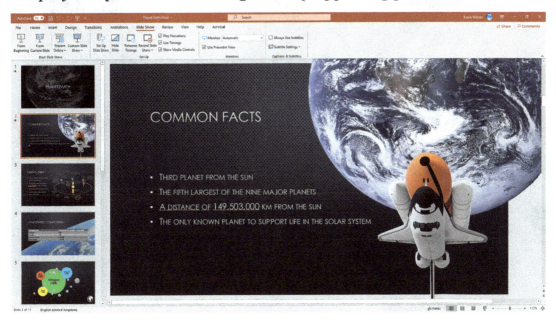

PowerPoint presentations consist of a series of slides. Each slide can contain multiple elements such as text, charts, tables, photographs, audio, and videos. Each of these elements can be animated to enhance audience engagement and understanding of the topic being presented. There is a library of animation and transition effects that can be applied to slides and individual elements within slides. These effects can help to emphasize key points and keep the audience engaged.

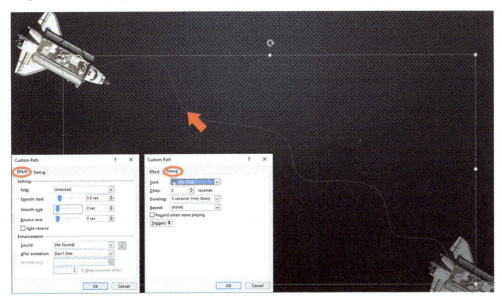

Chapter 1: Microsoft PowerPoint

You can run PowerPoint on various different platforms such as Windows, macOS, iPhone/iPad, Android, and in a web browser. Here in the demo below, we can see PowerPoint running on an iPhone.

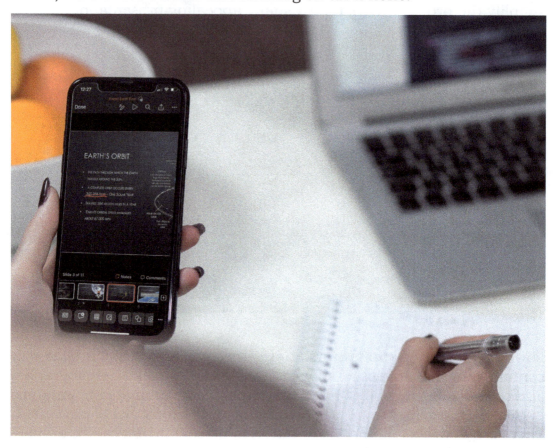

While PowerPoint for iPhone/iPad and Android offer great flexibility and convenience, they do have some limitations compared to the full-featured desktop version of PowerPoint available on Windows and macOS. The app doesn't include all the advanced features and tools available in the desktop version, such as detailed customization options for animations and slide transitions, or advanced data integration features for charts.

Also given the smaller screen size of smart phones and tablets compared to desktop monitors, the user interface is more condensed, which can limit ease of use or accessibility of certain features.

Using PowerPoint in a web browser onlinbe does not offer the full range of features and customization options available in the desktop version. This includes some advanced animation and transition options, certain complex chart types, and detailed data integration tools.

However, the iPhone/iPad and Android app is useful for editing presentations on the go.

You can link your laptop or tablet to a digital projector or large TV. PowerPoint provides a set of tools specifically designed for presenters, including Presenter View, which displays the current slide, speaker notes, and a preview of the next slide on the presenter's screen while the audience only sees the current slide. This feature helps presenters deliver their presentations more effectively and smoothly.

PowerPoint integrates seamlessly with other Microsoft Office applications such as Word and Excel. This allows you to easily add charts, tables, and text from these applications maintaining data consistency and efficiency in creating complex presentations.

There are also various collaboration features that enable multiple users to work on the same presentation simultaneously. Users can share presentations via email, cloud storage services, or SharePoint, and they can also export presentations to various formats such as PDF or video for easy distribution.

2

Getting Started

In this chapter, we'll explore the functionalities and mechanics of the Microsoft PowerPoint interface We'll look at:

- Getting Started
- Create a Shortcut
- The Ribbon
- File Backstage
- Normal View
- Outline View
- Slide Sorter View
- Note Page View
- Quick Access Toolbar
- File Types

To help you better understand this section, take a look at the video resources. Open your web browser and navigate to the following website:

elluminetpress.com/ppt-start

Getting Started

You can start PowerPoint by searching for it using Cortana's search field on your task bar. Type in 'powerpoint'. Then click 'PowerPoint ' desktop app as highlighted below.

Create a Shortcut

To make things easier, you can pin the PowerPoint icon to your task bar. I find this feature useful. To do this, right click on the PowerPoint icon on your taskbar and click 'pin to taskbar'.

This way, PowerPoint is always on the taskbar whenever you need it.

Chapter 2: Getting Started

Once PowerPoint has started, you'll land on the home screen. On the home screen, you'll see recently used templates along the top, and your most recently saved presentations listed underneath.

To begin, click 'new' to start. Here you'll find templates and pre-designed themes to help you create your presentation.

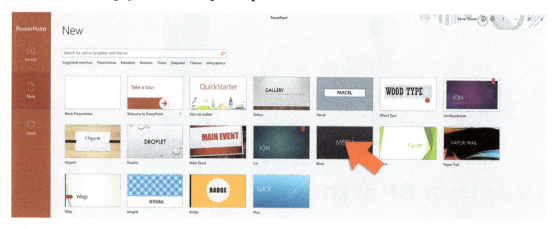

On some templates, you can choose color schemes and styles for fonts and text. The mesh template has 4 different color schemes which affect the color of the text. Click on one and click create.

Lets take a look at PowerPoint's main screen. Along the top are your ribbon menu. This is where you'll find all your tools for creating your slides.

Down the left hand side, you'll see a thumbnail list of all your slides in the presentation, in the centre of the screen you'll see the currently selected slide you're working on.

Along the bottom right you'll see icons to add presenter notes and comments. Adjust the view - ie how PowerPoint displays your slides on your screen. You can have normal view, slide sorter view and reading view. The next icon along runs your presentation - use this when presenting to your audience.

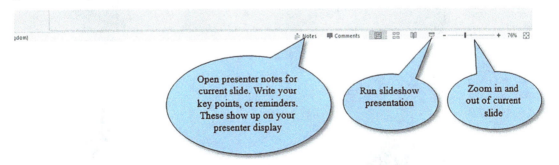

You can also adjust the zoom. This zooms in and out of the current slide. The last icon auto fits the current slide to the same size as the screen.

Speaker notes. These aren't visible to your audience, but will show up on the presenter view while you give your presentation.

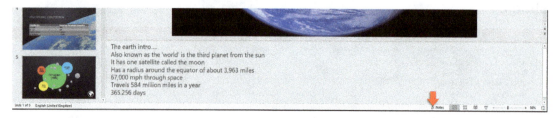

Slide sorter view. Click and drag slides to reorder.

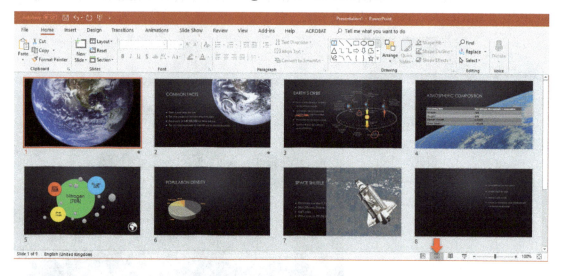

Normal view. Best view for designing your PowerPoint presentations.

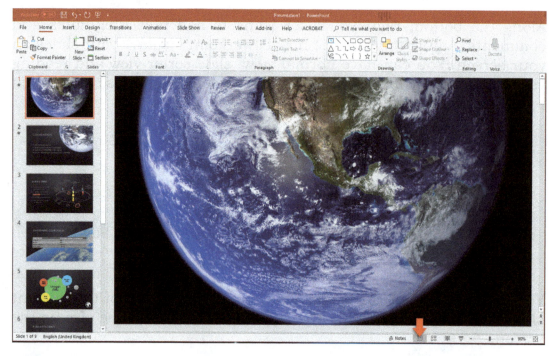

The Ribbon

All tools in PowerPoint are organised into a ribbon which is divided into ribbon tabs, each containing a specific set of tools.

Home Ribbon Tab

All tools to do with text formatting, for example, making text bold, changing fonts, and the most common tools for text alignment, and formatting.

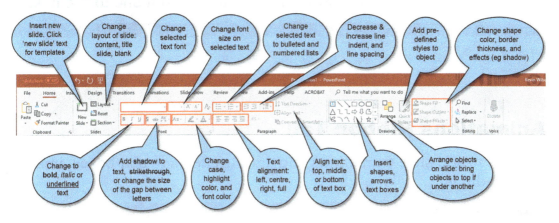

You'll also find your cut, copy & paste functions, as well as shortcuts for adding shapes, and inserting new slides.

Insert Ribbon Tab

All tools to do with inserting photos, graphics, 3D models, tables, charts, sounds, or movies. You can also insert equations, word art and smart art using this ribbon.

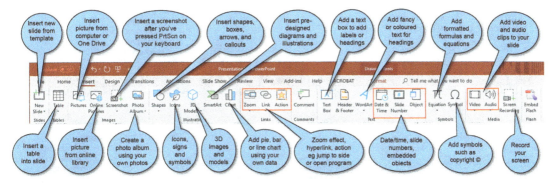

You can create zoom effects to help emphasise an illustration on your slide, as well as screen recordings, and on click actions.

Design Ribbon Tab

All tools to do with the look of your slide, eg, the slide background.

Transitions Ribbon Tab

All tools to add effects to show as slides change from one to the next.

Animations Ribbon Tab

All tools to add slide transitions and adding effects to text boxes, images and headings.

Slide Show Ribbon Tab

All tools to do with setting up your slide show and running your presentation.

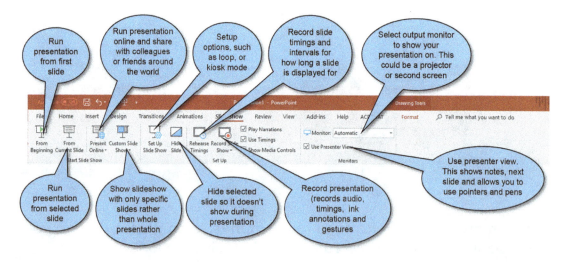

File Backstage

If you click 'File' on the top left of your screen, this will open up what Microsoft call the backstage.

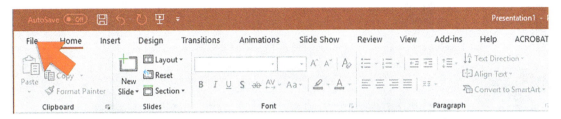

Backstage is where you open or save presentations, print, export or share presentations, as well as options, Microsoft account and preference settings.

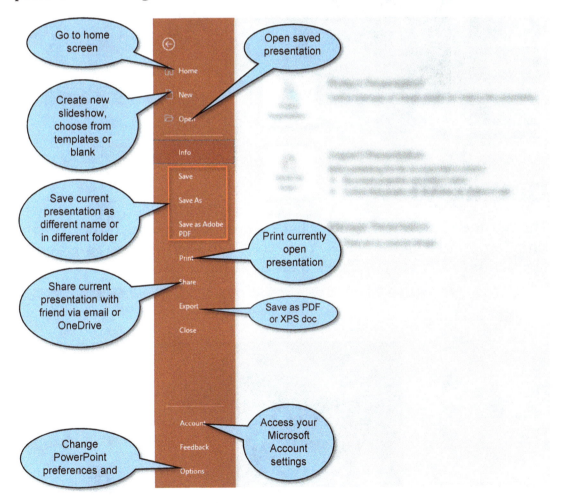

You can also change your Microsoft Account settings, log in and activate your Microsoft Office, change PowerPoint's preferences and so on.

Normal View

Normal view is the default view and the best way to design and develop your presentation. It lists all your slides down the left hand side, with the selected slide displayed in the centre of the screen for you to work on.

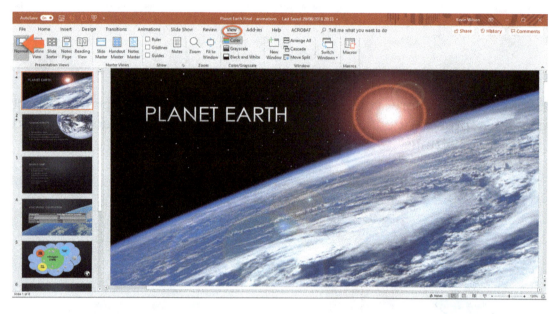

Outline View

The outline view, shows you a list of your slide's text, rather than a thumbnail view of the slide. You wont see any images or graphics inserted into any of your slides on the left hand side.

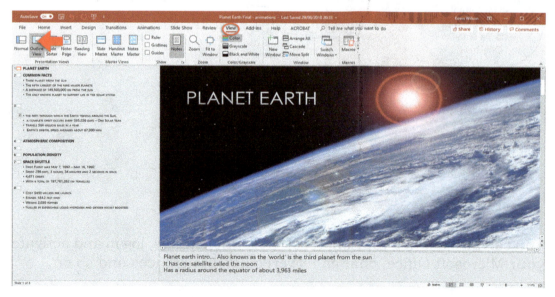

Slide Sorter View

The slide sorter view shows you a thumbnail list of all your slides in the presentation.

As the name suggests, it allows you to easily see all your slides and makes it easier for you to put them into the correct order.

As well as hide certain slides you may not need in a particular session when presenting. To do this, right click the slide, then from the popup menu select 'hide slide'.

Hidden slides are greyed out with the slide number crossed out. To un-hide the slide, right click on the slide, and click 'hide slide' again.

Note Page View

Note page view, allows you to see the slide with the notes associated with that slide.

Select the view ribbon and click 'notes page'.

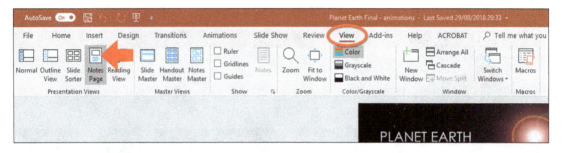

The notes view makes it easier to add notes to each slide, or to review notes already added.

Reading View

To switch to reading view, select the view ribbon and click 'reading view'.

This view allows you to play your PowerPoint presentation slideshow within the PowerPoint window.

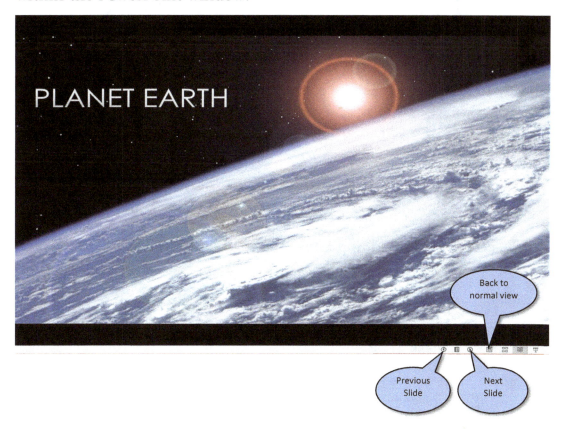

By using different page views, you can keep your presentation organized. For example, you can use the 'Slide Sorter' view to rearrange the order of your slides or the 'Outline' view to create a clear and logical structure for your presentation.

Additionally, by using the 'Notes Page' view, you can have notes and prompts on your presenter screen during your presentation. This way you won't need to stop and refer to your notes or other materials which can help your presentation flow more smoothly.

Quick Access Toolbar

The Quick Access Toolbar provides quick and easy access to frequently used commands and functions with just a click. You'll find it on the top left of the title bar in the main window.

By default, the Quick Access Toolbar contains only a few commonly used commands such as Save, Undo, and Redo.

If you want to add a command, right-click on any command in the ribbon then select 'Add to Quick Access Toolbar'. For example, if you wanted to add the 'new slide' command from the 'developer' ribbon.

You'll see the command appear on the toolbar.

If you want to remove a command, right-click on it and choose "Remove from Quick Access Toolbar."

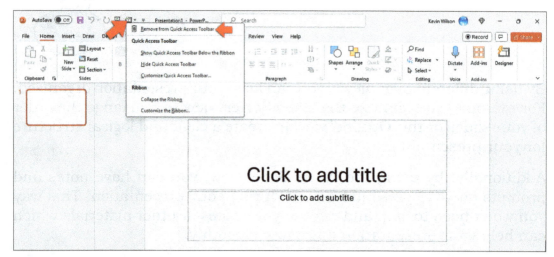

File Types

PowerPoint supports a variety of file types, each serving different purposes or compatibility needs.

.PPTX (PowerPoint Presentation) is the default file format for presentations created with PowerPoint 2007 and later versions. It uses the Open XML format, which allows for smaller file sizes and improved data management.

.PPT (PowerPoint 97-2003 Presentation) is compatible with earlier versions of PowerPoint, from 97 to 2003. While it can still be opened in newer versions of PowerPoint, some newer features might not be available or work as expected.

.POTX (PowerPoint Template) is used for templates rather than presentations. Templates can include themes, slide layouts, fonts, and colors that you can use as a starting point for creating new presentations.

.POT (PowerPoint 97-2003 Template) is the template format for PowerPoint 97 to 2003. Like .POTX, it's used for creating new presentations with a consistent design but is compatible with older versions of PowerPoint.

.PPSX (PowerPoint Show) is used for presentations that are intended to be viewed immediately as a slideshow, rather than for editing. When you double-click a .PPSX file, PowerPoint opens in slideshow mode.

.PPS (PowerPoint 97-2003 Show) is similar to .PPSX format and is for slideshow files compatible with PowerPoint 97 to 2003.

.PPAM (PowerPoint Add-In) extends PowerPoint's functionality with additional features, such as custom commands or specialized tasks. This format is used to store these add-ins.

.PPTM, .POTM, .PPSM (Macro-Enabled File Types) are similar to .PPTX, .POTX, and .PPSX respectively, but they allow for the inclusion of macros. Macros are scripts that can automate repetitive tasks or extend PowerPoint's capabilities.

.THMX (Theme File) is a theme file that stores colors, fonts, and effects. Themes can be applied to presentations to ensure a consistent visual appearance.

.ODP (OpenDocument Presentation) is used by some other office suites, like LibreOffice and OpenOffice. PowerPoint can open and save to this format, offering some level of cross-compatibility.

3

Building Presenta- tions

In this chapter, we'll explore how to create presentations, edit and format text. We'll look at:

- Building Presentations
- Creating a New Presentation
- Editing a Slide
- Adding a New Slide
- Advanced Text Editing
- Text Boxes
- Changing the Slide Order
- Slide Themes
- Slide Sizes
- Using the Selection Pane
- Slide Backgrounds
- Slide Headers & Footers
- Slide Masters
- Slide Templates
- Adding Notes
- Copying, Duplicating & Deleting Slides

To help you better understand this section, take a look at the video resources. Open your web browser and navigate to the following website:

elluminetpress.com/ppt-build

You'll also need to download the source files from:

elluminetpress.com/ppt

Creating a New Presentation

When you launch PowerPoint, you're greeted with the home screen. This displays your most frequently used PowerPoint templates at the top, and below, a list of your most recently accessed presentations.

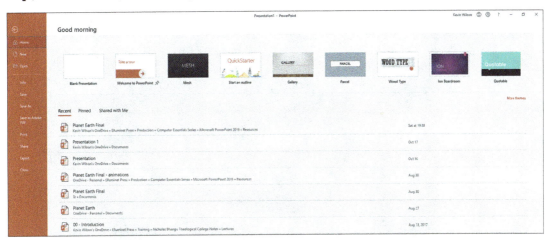

PowerPoint provides an extensive library of templates and themes suitable for various presentation types. To access these templates, select 'New' from the orange navigation pane on the left side of the screen.

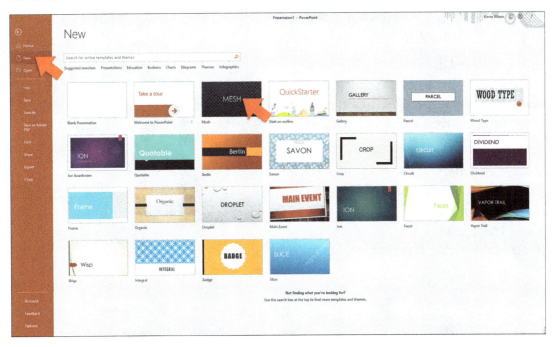

To begin building a presentation, select 'blank presentation' to create a presentation from scratch, or select a template. For this example I'm going to use the 'mesh' template, but you can choose any one you like.

After selecting a template, PowerPoint will add a title slide for you. This is shown in the main area of the screen and is where you can enter the title of your presentation and a subtitle or your name if needed.

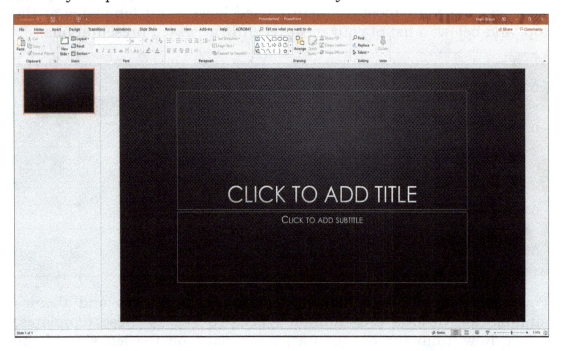

The panel on the left of the main screen is called the thumbnail pane. This displays miniature versions of the slides in the order they will appear in the presentation.

You can use this panel to quickly navigate between different slides in your presentation. Or rearrange slides by clicking and dragging them to a new position.

You can also select slides to duplicate or delete them. To do this, just right click on the slide then select 'delete slide' or 'duplicate slide' from the popup menu.

Each template comes with a set of pre-designed slide layouts and theme elements, ensuring your presentation has a consistent and professional look throughout.

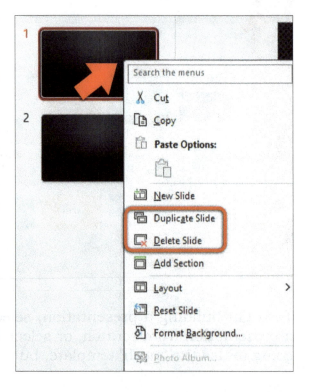

Editing a Slide

Lets begin by adding the title to our first slide. On the slide, click where it says 'click to add title'. This is a place holder for you to enter a title.

Type in the title 'Planet Earth'.

In this example, we won't be adding a subtitle, but you can add one if you want to. If you want to add a subtitle, click where it says 'click to add subtitle', then type in your subtitle.

Adding a New Slide

To continue building our presentation we need additional slides to show our information. To add a new slide, go to the home ribbon tab then click on icon 'New Slide'. Make sure you click on the text to reveal the drop down menu. There are various different slide layouts you can choose from. These can change depending on the template or theme you choose.

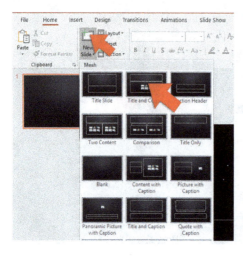

Title Slide is the first slide in a presentation, usually including the presentation's title and the presenter's name.

Title and Content is a common slide layout that includes a title at the top and a space for content such as text, images, charts, etc.

Section Header is usually used to introduce a new section or topic within the presentation.

Two Content divides the slide into two sections for content, typically used for comparison or displaying two related sets of information.

Comparison is similar to the Two Content layout, but it is specifically designed to compare two different items or sets of data.

Title Only provides a title with a blank space for content that doesn't fit the standard layouts.

Blank inserts an empty slide with no placeholders.

Content with Caption features a large content area with a space for a caption or brief description.

Picture with Caption is a layout designed for showcasing an image with a description or caption.

Panoramic Picture with Caption is tailored for a wide image, likely spanning the whole slide width, with a caption area.

Title and Caption is a simple layout with a title and a separate space for a caption or subtitle.

Quote with Caption is deal for when you need to display a quote and its source or a related comment.

In this example I'm going to select 'title and content' because I want a title on the slide and somesome information in bullet points in the main body of the slide.

To add your text and titles, just click in the text boxes and start typing your information as shown below.

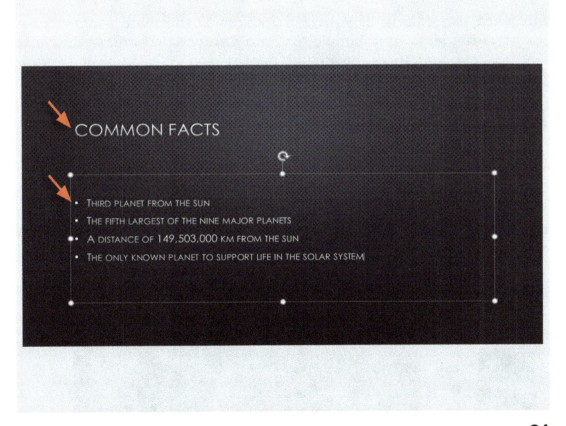

You can make text bigger by selecting it. Drag and highlight the text. From your home ribbon select the increase font size icon.

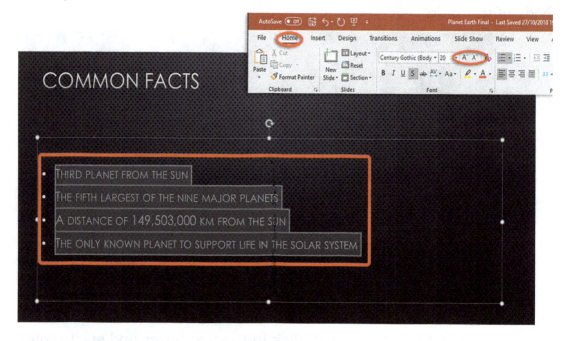

Advanced Text Editing

Advanced text editing in PowerPoint refers to the more sophisticated features that go beyond simple text entry and basic formatting. These features can enhance the visual appeal and effectiveness of your presentation

Character Spacing

Adjust the space between characters, also known as kerning, for a more polished look, especially at larger font sizes.

Select the text you want to modify. On the 'home' ribbon tab, click on the small icon on the bottom-right of the 'font' group to open the font dialog box.

Go to the Character Spacing tab. Choose the spacing option you want (Normal, Expanded, Condensed) and adjust the point value if necessary.

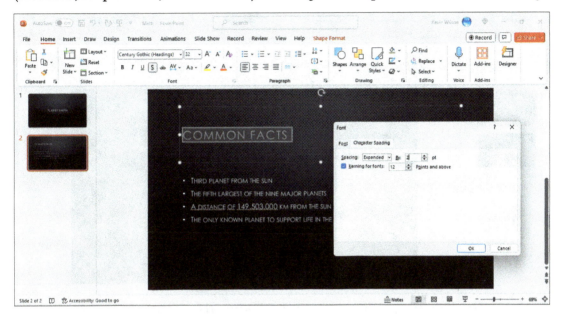

Spacing dropdown menu allows you to choose the type of character spacing. The option shown is "Expanded," which means that space will be added between the characters. Other options include "Normal" and "Condensed". Normal is the default spacing setting that does not add or subtract space between characters. Condensed is opposite to expanded, this setting reduces the space between characters.

By field lets you specify exactly how much space you want to add (when expanded) or remove (when condensed) between characters.

Kerning for fonts adjusts the space between specific pairs of characters to make the spacing more uniform. It's typically used for larger font sizes to improve the visual appearance of the text.

Points and above box allows you to enter a font size threshold at which kerning will be applied. In the screenshot above, kerning is set to apply to fonts that are 12 points or larger.

Click 'ok' when you're done.

Text Direction

Changes the orientation of text, allowing it to be rotated or stacked, which is useful for labels on vertical axes in graphs or for text in narrow columns.

Select the text box containing the text you want to rotate. From the 'home' ribbon tab, click on 'text direction' in the 'paragraph' group.

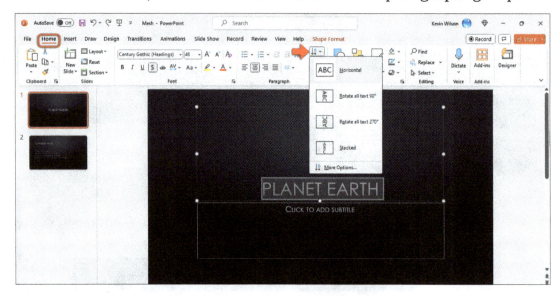

Choose the direction that suits your design (Horizontal, Rotate all text 90°, Rotate all text 270°, Stacked).

Bullets and Numbering

You can customize the style, color, and size of bullet points or numbers to match your presentation's theme and enhance readability. To do this select the text you want to format with bullets or numbering.

From the 'home' ribbon tab, in the Paragraph group, choose either the Bullets or Numbering button to apply the default style.

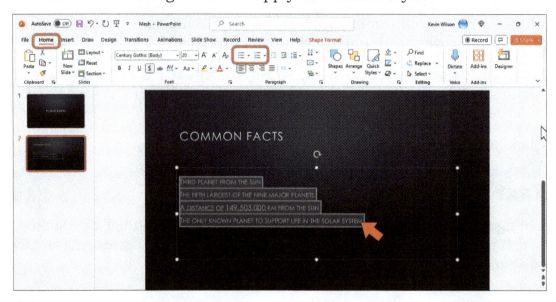

To customize the bullets or numbering styles, click the small drop-down arrow next to the Bullets or Numbering icons to choose from more styles.

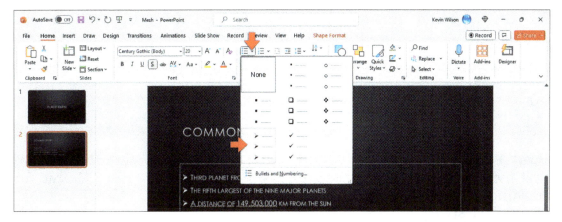

If you want to change the color or size, click 'bullets & numbering' at the bottom of the drop down menu. From the dialog box, select a style, size and color.

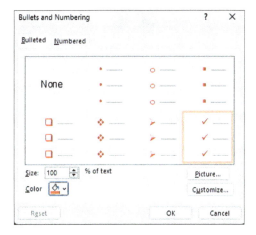

Size controls the size of the bullet relative to the text size. In this case, it's set to 100% of the text size.

Color paint bucket icon indicates that you can change the color of the bullets. Clicking this would likely bring up a color palette to choose from.

Picture allows you to replace the standard bullet with an image file, providing an option for custom bullets.

Customize allows you to choose from more characters you can use to create a custom bullet style.

Click 'ok' when you're done.

Font Styling

Utilize bold, italic, underline, and other font styles to draw attention or denote importance. To change the font, select the text you want to format. You can do this using the icons in the 'font' group on the 'home' ribbon tab.

Font Family Dropdown currenty set to "Century Gothic (Headings)" text indicates that the current font family is set to Century Gothic for headings. Clicking the dropdown arrow allows you to change the font to another style.

Font Size Dropdown currenty set at "32" this shows the font size. You can click on this to select a different font size or type a custom size into the box.

Increase Font Size icon with an up arrow will increase the font size incrementally.

Decrease Font Size icon with a down arrow will decrease the font size incrementally.

Clear Formatting "A icon with an eraser next to it will clear all the formatting from the selected text, reverting to the default font style.

Bold "B" icon will make the selected text bold.

Italic "I" icon will italicize the selected text.

Underline "U" icon will underline the selected text.

Strikethrough "ab" icon will apply a strikethrough effect to the selected text.

Character Spacing "AV" icon will adjust the spacing between characters.

Change Case "Aa" icon will allow you to change the case of the selected text to all caps, all lower case, or sentense case.

Text Highlight pen icon with a color bar below it is for highlighting text. Clicking it once will apply the highlight; clicking the dropdown arrow will allow you to change the highlight color.

Font Color "A" icon with a color bar below it is used to change the color of the selected text. The dropdown arrow next to it likely provides access to more color options.

To get more font options, click the small icon on the bottom right of the 'font' group.

Here you can adjust the font size and style, as well as other effects such as strikethrough, subscript and superscipt.

Alignment and Indentation

You can fine-tune the alignment of text within a text box, adjust the indentation of paragraphs, and set tabs for a consistent look.

Alignment

Select the text within a text box that you want to align. From the 'home' ribbon tab, in the Paragraph group, you'll see a set of alignment tools.

Align Text Left aligns the text to the left side of the text box.

Center aligns the text to the center of the text box.

Align Text Right aligns the text to the right side of the text box.

Justify spreads the text out evenly across the text box so both left and right margins are justified.

Indentation

Select the text you wish to indent. From the 'home' ribbon tab, in the 'paragraph' group, find buttons in increase or decrease selected text.

Increase Indent button moves the text further away from the left border of the text box. Each click increases the indent level.

Decrease Indent button moves the text closer to the left border of the text box. Each click reduces the indent level.

Line Spacing

You can control the amount of space between lines, which can affect readability and text density on a slide. To do this, select the text you want to adjust.

From the 'home' ribbon tab, in the Paragraph group, click on the Line Spacing icon.

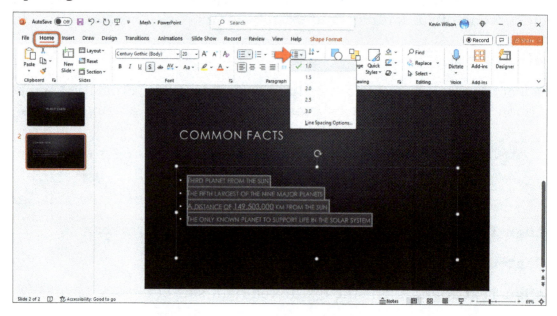

Choose from the list of predefined line spacing options, or select 'line spacing options' to enter a custom value.

Text Boxes

A text box is an object you can place on a slide to hold text. It's a rectangular box that acts as a container for word processing. You can adjust the internal margins within a text box to control the padding around text.You can also resize text boxes for better layout and design, and use text box resizing options to fit text or to shrink text on overflow.

Adding Text Boxes

To add a text box open your presentation and go to the slide where you want to add a text box. From the 'insert' ribbon tab, click on the Text Box button.

Your cursor will change to a downward-pointing arrow with a small text box icon. Click and drag to define the size of the text box you want to create.

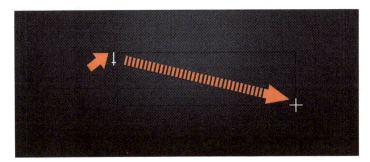

Once the text box appears, you can start typing your text immediately.

After typing your text, you can format it using the options in the 'home' ribbon tab. You can move and resize the text box as needed by clicking and dragging its edges or using the handles around the text box.

Slide Themes

You can select from a variety of themes. To do this select the 'design' ribbon. In the middle of the ribbon, you'll see some themes to choose from. Click the small down arrow on the right hand side of the 'themes' section to expand the selection.

Select a theme from the list.

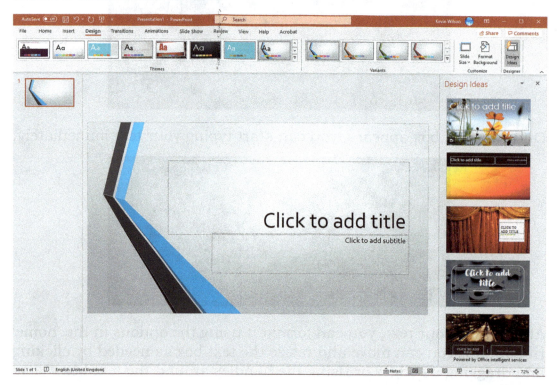

Slide Sizes

PowerPoint presentations come with default slide sizes, but there are situations where you might need to adjust these to fit different screens and projectors.

Standard Sizes

Widescreen (aspect ratio 16:9) is the default slide size for newer versions of PowerPoint. It fits most modern computer screens, projectors, and HDTV screens. Widescreen gives you more space horizontally, which is useful for more detailed slides or including side-by-side content.

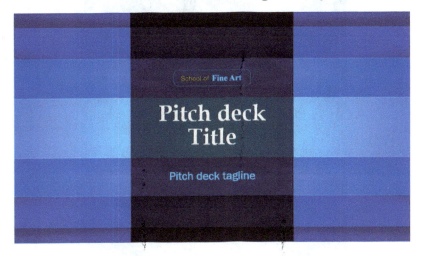

Standard (aspect ratio 4:3) was the default in older versions of PowerPoint. It's more square and can be a better choice for older projector screens, TVs and some tablet devices. While it offers less horizontal space, it can be ideal for presentations that will be viewed on older equipment or printed out on card or paper.

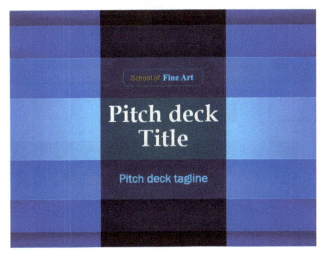

Custom Sizes

PowerPoint allows you to customize the slide size to fit specific requirements. Custom slide sizes can be particularly useful for creating digital signage, custom print layouts, or when the presentation will be displayed on a screen with an unusual aspect ratio.

For example, designing content for a instagram portrait post, which often has a wide aspect ratio such as 4:5 with dimensions of 1080 pixels x 1350 pixels (38.1 cm x 47.625 cm).

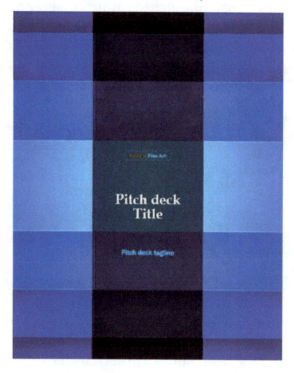

Changing the Slide Size

To change the size go to the 'design' ribbon tab. Click on 'Slide Size' near the far right end of the ribbon.

Select between standard or widescreen. Or if you need a different size select 'Custom Slide Size' from the dropdown menu.

In the 'Slide Size' dialog, you can choose from predefined sizes or enter your custom width and height. You can select the unit of measurement that suits your needs (e.g., inches, centimeters, pixels). Select a size from the 'slides sized for' drop down, or enter the exact width and height. Click 'ok' when you're done.

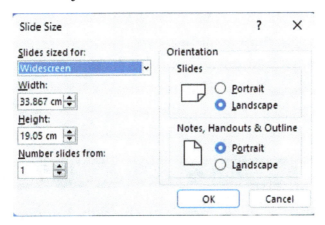

PowerPoint will ask whether you want to maximize the size of your existing content to fit the new slide size, or scale it down to ensure it fits within the new slide size.

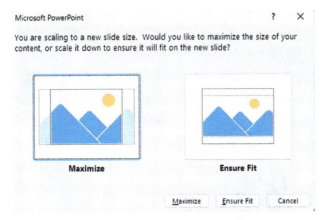

Maximize will increase the size of your content so that it fills the new slide size as much as possible without stretching it out of proportion. This might mean that some content will be cropped off the edges if the aspect ratio of the new slide size is different from the old one.

Ensure Fit will scale down your content to make sure that everything fits on the new slide size. This could result in more white space around your content, especially if the aspect ratio of the new slide size is different.

This dialog box helps to preserve the visual integrity of your slides when changing dimensions.

Using the Selection Pane

The Selection Pane in PowerPoint is a useful tool that allows you to manage all the objects on a slide. It's particularly helpful when you have multiple layers of text boxes, shapes, images, and other elements that might be difficult to select directly on the slide.

To do this, from the 'home' ribbon tab, click on 'select' in the 'editing' group. Choose 'selection pane' from the dropdown menu.

You'll see the selection pane appear on the right hand side of the screen. Each text box, title, chart or image is named and listed in the selection pane. And are listed in order from top to bottom. Objects are stacked on top of eachother so, "title 1" is at the bottom (or back) of the stack, and "Picture 4" is on the top (or front).

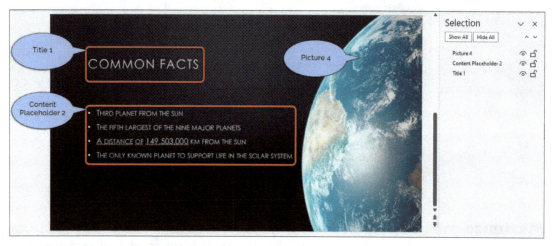

The "eye" icon next to each object allows you to toggle its visibility. Show or hide the object.

Double-click on an object's name in the pane to rename it. This can make it easier to keep track of slide elements, particularly when writing animations or triggers.

You can change the order in which objects are stacked by dragging them up or down in the list. Objects at the top of the list are in front, and those at the bottom are at the back.

Slide Backgrounds

PowerPoint provides several options for customizing slide backgrounds, allowing you to create visually appealing presentations that can emphasize your content and engage your audience.

Solid Fill fills your slide's background with a single color. This is effective for clean, minimalist designs.

Gradient Fill create a gradient that blends two or more colors. You can customize the direction, the type (linear or radial), and the transition of colors for a more dynamic background.

Picture allows you to insert an image from your computer or online sources to serve as the background.

Texture Fill allows you to use a predefined texture, or upload your own image to create a textured background.

Pattern Fill allows you to select from a variety of built-in patterns with adjustable foreground and background colors.

Changing the Background

To access and apply these background options, you can use the Format Background pane. From the 'design' ribbon tab, click on 'format background'.

The Format Background pane will appear on the right side of the screen.

Choose one of the fill options at the top of the panel: solid fill, gradient fill, picture or texture fill, or pattern fill.

Select **Solid Fill**, then click the "Color" button to open the color palette, where you can choose any color you want.

Select **Gradient Fill,** then choose the options to customise your gradient. Click on the 'preset gradients' dropdown menu to select from a variety of predefined gradient fills as your starting point. Choose the gradient type from the dropdown menu. Select the direction of the gradient from the available options. If you've chosen a Linear gradient, you can set the angle at which the gradient progresses across the slide. Gradient Stops are points along the gradient line where you can specify colors and transitions. To add a new gradient stop, click on  the "+" button. To remove a gradient stop, click on it to select it and then press the "x" button. Click on a gradient stop to select it, then move it along the slider to change its position. Once you've selected a gradient stop, click on the "Color" button to choose a color for that stop. A color palette will appear for you to make your selection. Position specifies the location of the selected gradient stop along the gradient bar. You can move it by typing a percentage or using the slider. Transparency adjust the transparency of the selected gradient stop. A higher percentage will make the color more transparent. Brightness adjust the brightness of the selected gradient stop to make the color brighter or darker.

Select **Picture** to use an image as your background. Under "'Picture Source", click "Insert" to browse for and select the image you want to use. You can select and image from your computer, or you can select from various stock and online photos.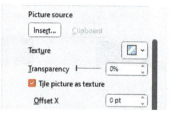

Select **Pattern Fill** to apply a two-color pattern to your slide background. Select your desired pattern from the list of available options that appear underneath.

This will apply the background settings to the currently selected slide. If you want to apply these settings to all the slides in your  presentation, click on "apply to all" at the bottom of the panel. Click 'reset background' to reset back to what it was.

Slide Headers & Footers

Slide headers and footers in PowerPoint are areas where you can include information that you want to repeat on each slide, like page numbers, the date and time, footer text, and even a logo or other image

Adding Headers and Footers to Slides

To add a header, go to the 'insert' ribbon tab, then click on 'Header & Footer' in the Text group.

A dialog box will open with options for the header and footer. Select the 'slides tab'. Select 'date and time' to add the date/time to each slide, click 'slide number' to add the slide numbers to each slide, click 'footer' then enter some text if you want a footer on each slide.

Date and Time allows you to include the current date and time on each slide, or a fixed date that you enter. There is also an option to update it automatically each time you open the presentation.

Slide Number, check this box to include slide numbers on each slide.

Footer is a text field where you can enter any text you want to appear on each slide, like a copyright notice, company name, or presentation title.

Don't Show on Title Slide will not include the header and footer on the title slide of your presentation.

Once you've made your choices, click on 'Apply to All' to add the header and footer to every slide, or select 'Apply' if you want it to only apply to the selected slides.

Slide Masters

Slide Masters allows you to design and apply consistent layouts across all the slides in your presentation. They act as a blueprint for your slides, ensuring uniformity in design, layout, and formatting. By editing a Slide Master, you can set the default styles for text (including fonts, sizes, and colors), backgrounds, logos, and other common elements. This efficiency is particularly beneficial for creating professional and cohesive presentations without having to manually format each slide.

Slide Masters are arranged into a hierarchy that structures how design elements and formatting rules are applied across your slides. At the top of the hierarchy is the Slide Master itself. It controls the global design elements of your presentation, including:

- Background styles (colors, images, gradients)
- Default font styles for titles and body text
- Color schemes
- Placeholder sizes and positions
- Footer, header, and date settings

Below the Slide Master are Layout Masters or Layout Slides each defining a specific slide layout within the Slide Master. These show up in the 'New Slide' drop down menu. PowerPoint offers a variety of predefined layouts, such as:

- Title Slide
- Title and Content
- Section Header
- Two Content
- Content with Caption

For example, if you are creating a presentation and want a company logo on the bottom, you can add it to your slide master and the logo will appear on every slide you create.

To edit your slide masters, go to your view ribbon and click 'slide master'.

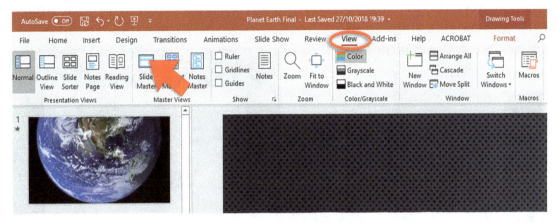

The larger slide listed down the left hand side is your master for all slides. The smaller ones are layout masters for individual slide layouts such as 'title slides' or 'title and content' slides. These appear in the 'new slide' drop down menu. You can split them up so you can create templates for specific slides.

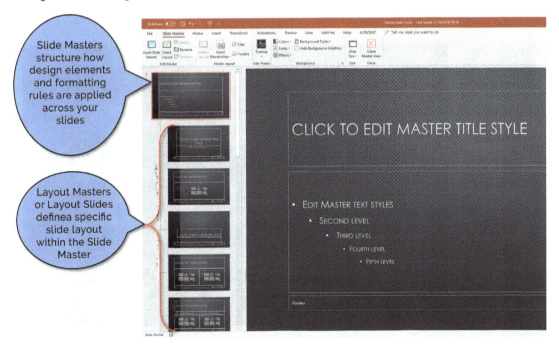

Slide Masters structure how design elements and formatting rules are applied across your slides

Layout Masters or Layout Slides definea specific slide layout within the Slide Master

This way, you can have consistent layouts for all your title slides and all your content slides, without having to change the size of the title or position of text or the font every time you insert a new slide.

In this simple example, I am going to add the company logo to the bottom right of every slide. To do this, click on the larger master slide in the list on the left hand side.

Open your file explorer and navigate to your pictures folder, or the folder where the picture you want is saved. Click and drag your image onto the master slide.

You may need to resize your picture and position it in the correct place.

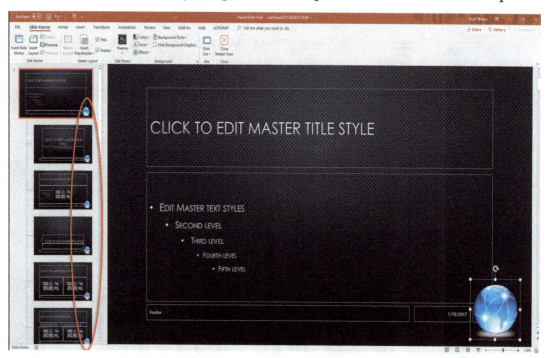

Notice, when you add the logo to the larger slide, it appears on the smaller slides too. This is because the smaller slides inherit their formatting from the larger slide (the larger slide being the parent master slide).

If specific slides (such as the title slide or section header slide) require unique formatting, select the respective layout from the left pane and make the adjustments. For instance, you might want a larger font for the title slide or a different background color for section headers.

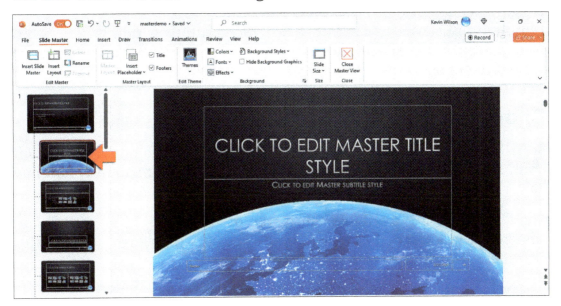

When you're finished click 'close master view'.

Now, whenever you add a new slide to your presentation, it will automatically feature the company logo in the bottom right corner, and any text you add to the title or content placeholders will adhere to the default fonts and sizes you've set. This ensures that your presentation remains consistent in terms of branding and style, no matter how many slides you add or how many different people contribute to the presentation.

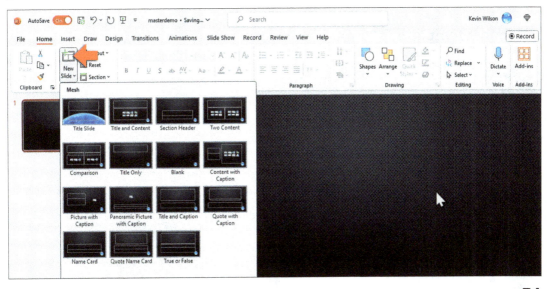

Slide Templates

Slide templates are pre-designed layouts that provide a consistent structure and look for the content on your slides. They can include preset placeholders for text, images, charts, shapes, and backgrounds. Templates serve as a starting point for creating a new slide within your presentation, ensuring uniformity and a professional appearance across all slides.

Choosing a Template

Start by launching PowerPoint. Select 'new' from the panel on the left hand side. You can also select 'file' then 'new', if you're already running PowerPoint.

Scroll through the available templates or use the search bar to find something more specific. PowerPoint offers a wide range of templates for different purposes and styles.

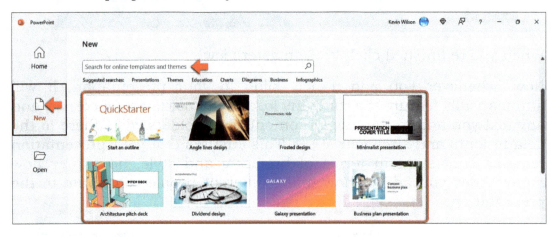

Click on a template that you like to see a preview and a brief description of it. When you find one that suits your needs, click the "create" button to open a new presentation based on that template.

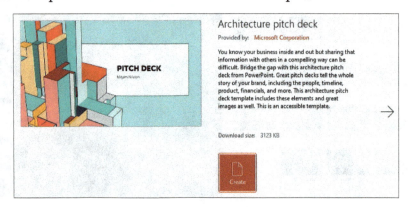

Customizing a Template

Once you have selected a template, you'll see pre-defined slides down the left hand side of the screen in the slide navigation pane. You can change the layout of a specific slide to better suit your content. To do this, right-click on the slide in the slide navigation pane, choose "Layout," and then select the layout that best fits your needs.

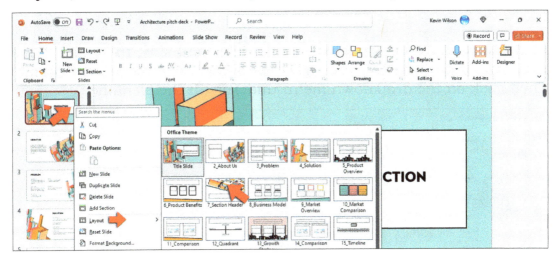

On each pre-defined slide, you'll see either example text, or placeholders. Click on any text box or placeholder to add your own content.

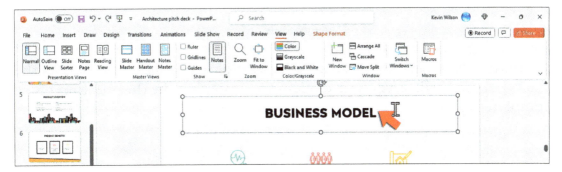

To change the overall design (like colors and fonts), go to the "Design" ribbon tab. Here, you can choose from different theme variations or customize the theme colors and fonts to your liking.

Saving Custom Templates

If you've made a presentation that you'd like to save as a template for future use, click "File" on the top left of the screen.

Select "Save As" from the panel on the left hand side, then click "This PC". On the "Save As" page, give the template a meaningful name. Then click on the drop down menu underneath the filename.

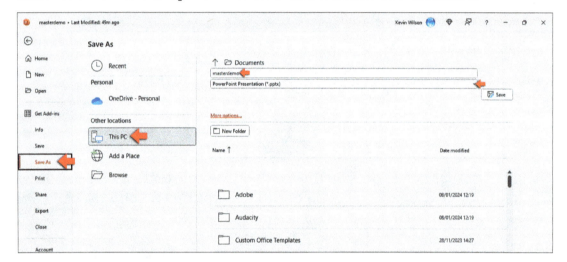

From the drop down menu, select "PowerPoint Template (*.potx)" as the file type. This will save your design as a template in the 'custom office templates' folder.

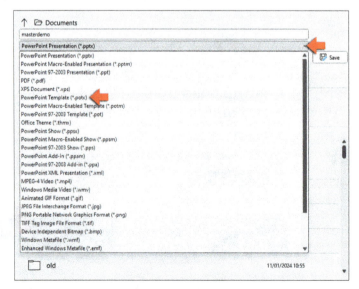

Using a Custom Template

To use your custom template, start PowerPoint, select 'new' from the panel on the left hand side. At the bottom of the page, click on the "Personal" link beside "Office" to see your custom templates saved in 'custom office templates' folder. Click on the template to open a new presentation.

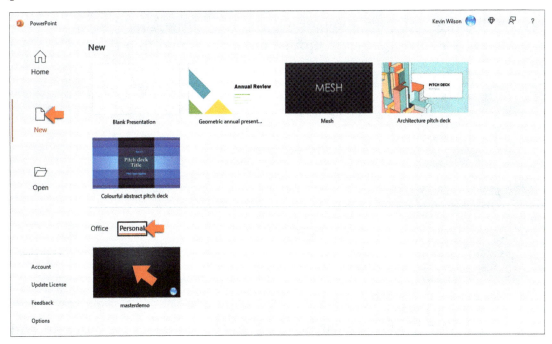

Click create.

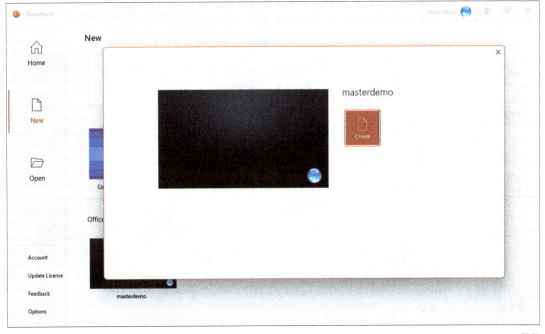

Adding Notes

You can add speakers notes to your slides. These notes appear on the presenter view when running your presentation. They can also appear on printed handouts.

First reveal the notes pane. The notes pane is located at the bottom of your screen, but is usually hidden by default. To reveal the pane, click on the dividing line just above the scroll bar, illustrated below with the red arrow. You'll notice your mouse cursor change to a double headed arrow.

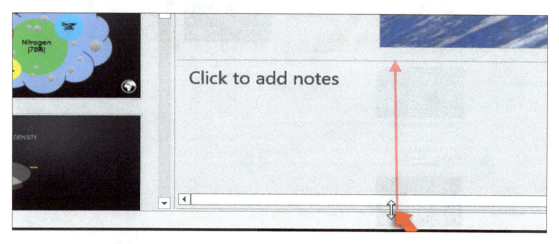

Then drag your mouse upwards to reveal the notes pane. You can add speakers notes, bullet points to help you when you're presenting.

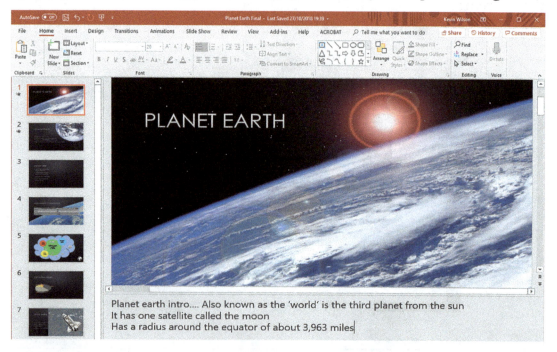

These notes will appear on your presenter view, when you run your presentation.

You can also include your notes in printed slide handouts. Go to FILE, then select print. Change the option, circled below, to 'Notes Pages'.

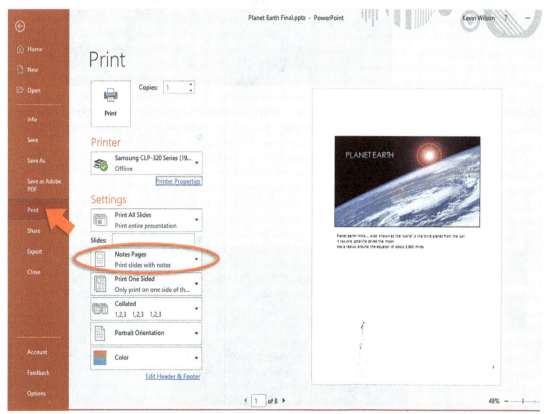

Managing Slides

Managing slides in PowerPoint involves several fundamental actions like copying, duplicating, and deleting slides. These actions allow you to efficiently organize and refine your presentations.

Copying Slides

Copying slides is useful when you want to use the same slide in different parts of your presentation or in a different presentation. To do this Right-click on the slide you want to copy in the panel on the left hand side, choose "Copy" from the popup menu. For example, I'm going to copy the first slide.

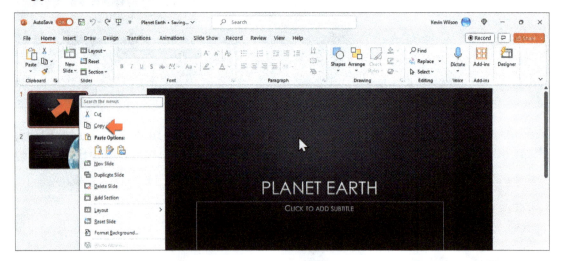

Right-click where you want to place the copied slide and select "Paste". For example at the end. You can paste the slide into the same presentation, or a different one.

Duplicating Slides

Duplicating is similar to copying but is inserts the duplicate straight after the slide being duplicated.

To do this, right-click on the slide you want to duplicate in the panel on the left. Select "Duplicate Slide" from the popup menu.

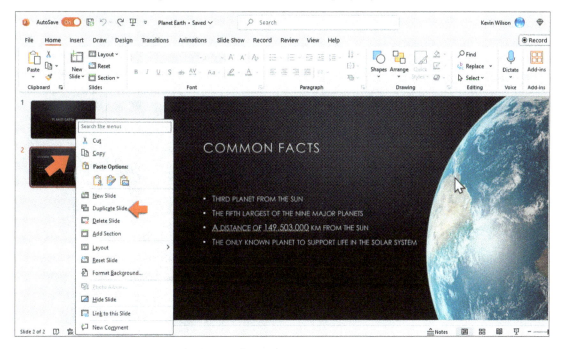

You'll see the duplicated slide appear immediately after the one being duplicated.

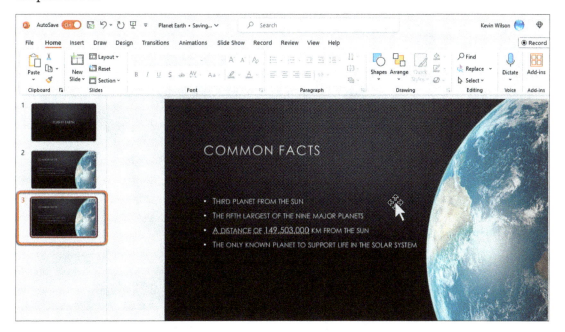

Deleting Slides

Deleting slides removes them from your presentation, useful for eliminating unnecessary or redundant information.

To do this, right-click on the slide you want to delete in the panel on the left hand side. Select "Delete Slide" from the popup menu.

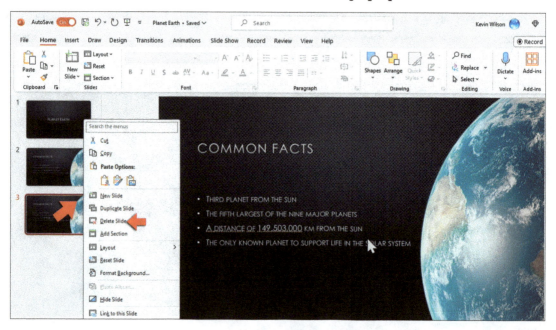

You'll see the slide you deleted will disappear from the panel on the left hand side.

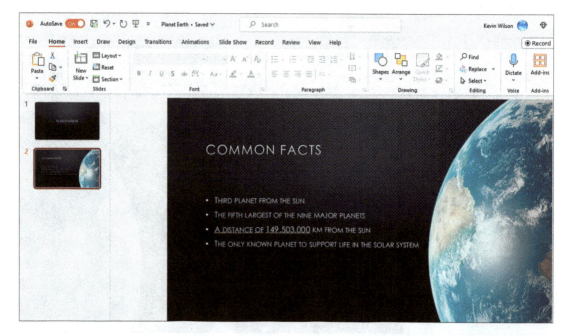

Changing the Slide Order

You can easily change the order or the slides in your presentation. To do this, on the left hand side of your screen, click and drag the slide thumbnails.

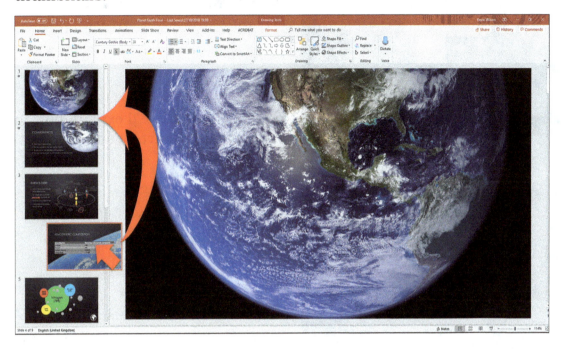

You'll see the other slides shift out the way. Drop the slide into the position you want.

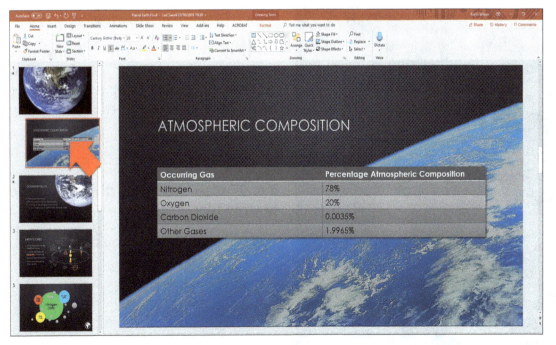

Adding Graphics

In this chapter, we'll explore how to add images, SmartArt and WordArt. We'll look at:

- Adding Images
- Design Ideas
- Adding Objects
- SmartArt
- WordArt
- Using 3D Models
- Adding Animation to 3D Models
- Custom Shapes
- Freeform Drawing

To help you better understand this section, take a look at the video resources. Open your web browser and navigate to the following website:

elluminetpress.com/ppt-grap

You'll also need to download the source files from:

elluminetpress.com/ppt

Adding Images

You can add images or photographs from your computer, for example, photos you have taken. Or you can add images from Office's online library and stock images library.

From your PC

The easiest way to add an image to your slide, is to first find the image in your pictures library from file explorer. The icon is on your task bar.

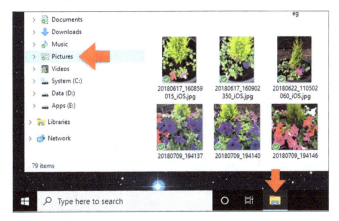

Open up your pictures library, then drag and drop the image onto your open slide, as shown below.

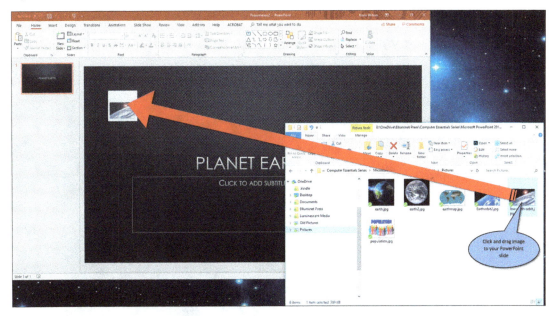

You may need to move your explorer window over to the side if it covers your PowerPoint presentation.

Online Images

You can also add pictures from Bing Images. From your insert ribbon, click 'pictures', then select 'online pictures'.

From the dialog box that appears, type your search into the Bing images field and press enter.

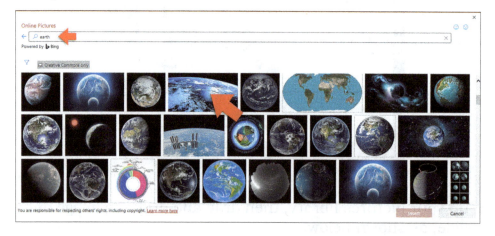

From the search results, click the image you want, then click 'insert'.

Now you can place your image and resize it to fit on your slide.

Stock Images

Microsoft have recently added royalty free stock images to their library. To add a stock image, go to the insert ribbon and click 'pictures'. Select 'stock images'.

Here you can download all sorts of stock images. Along the top of the window you'll see some categories.

Stock images contains a general image library you can search. Browse through the images or type your search into the search field at the top of the screen

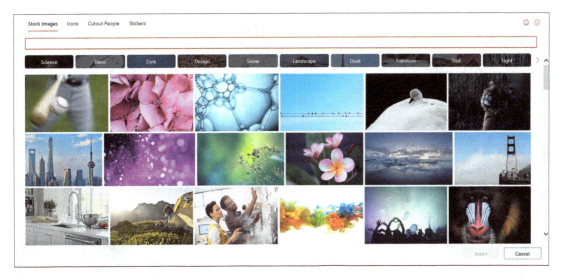

Click the image in the search results then click 'insert'.

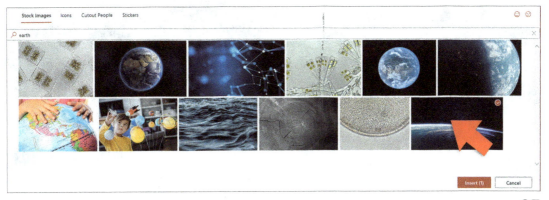

Chapter 4: Adding Graphics

Icons contains small pictures and symbols you can use to illustrate different ideas in your presentations.

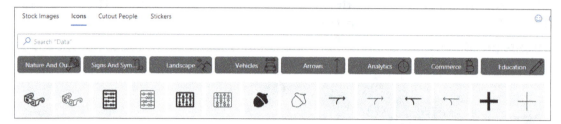

Cutout people is a library of people shot against a transparent background meaning you can insert them into your presentation without a background.

Stickers are little characters you can insert into your work.

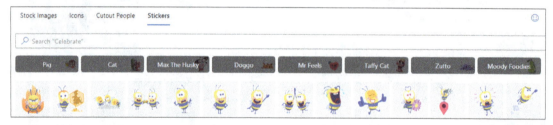

Select the 'stickers' category then select a sticker to add to your slide.

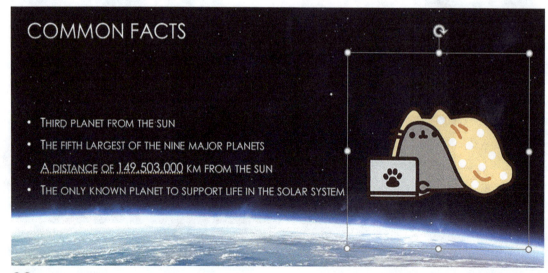

Resizing Images

If you click on your image, you will notice a border surrounding it.

In each corner and along the sides you will notice little white dots.

These are resize handles. You can click and drag these to resize your image.

To resize the image, click and drag the resize handles until the image is the size you want.

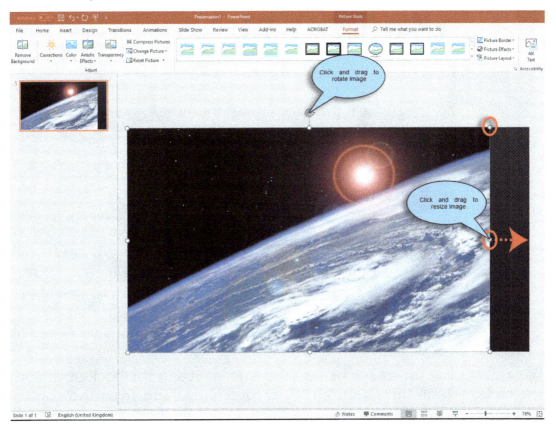

Image Arrangement

You will notice that when you have resized the image, it covers the title. This is because PowerPoint constructs slides using layers. So the title "Planet Earth" will be on one layer, and the image will be on another layer. Now, because the image was inserted after the title, the image layer is on top of the title layer. We want the title layer on top.

We can adjust this by changing the arrangement.

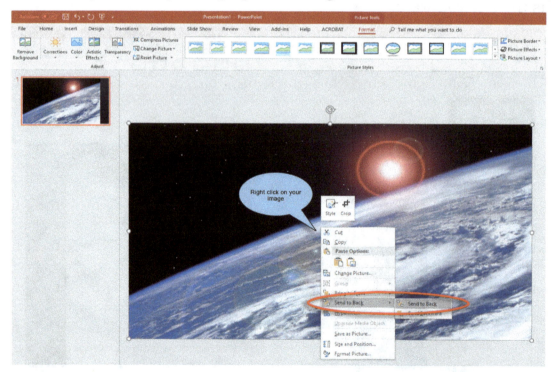

We want to put the image behind the title, so it's in the background on the slide. To do this, right click on your image and from the pop up menu, select 'send to back'.

You will see the image drop behind the text layer.

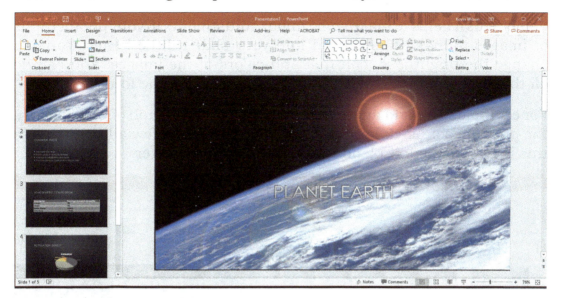

This is useful if you have a lot of images and text that you need to lay out on your slide.

You can now type the title 'Planet Earth' in the text box, and drag it to the desired position on the slide.

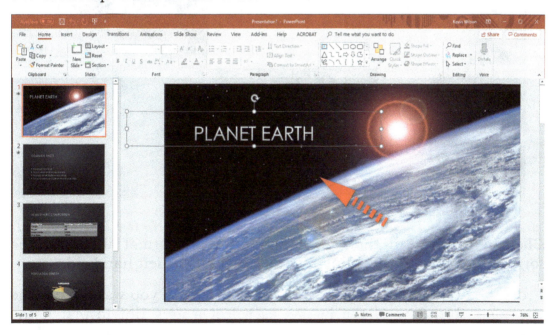

In my example, I'm going to put the title in the top left of the slide against the black. To drag the title text box, when you click on it, you'll see a box appear around the title text box. Click and drag the dotted line surrounding the title, to move your image.

Adjusting Images

Sometimes it helps to make some minor adjustments to your photographs or images to make them blend into your slide a little better. You can change the brightness, contrast and colors of the images. You can do all this by experimenting with the adjustments on the format ribbon.

For example. If we add another slide with the photograph of planet earth, the photo has a black background. We can make a few adjustments to this image to make it blend into the slide a little better.

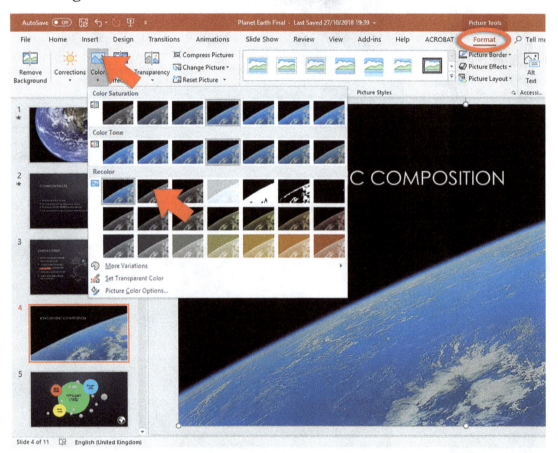

Click on the image on the slide and then click the format ribbon. On the format ribbon go to the adjustment section on the left hand side.

From the drop down menu, you can select 'color' if you want to change the color blending of the image, eg select a grey tint to match the background theme of the slide.

You can also do the same for other corrections such as brightness and contrast. Do this by selecting 'corrections' from the format ribbon instead of 'color'.

Removing Image Backgrounds

This works best on images that don't have complex or crowded backgrounds.

Instead of seeing the black background from the image, it would be better to use the slide background itself, rather than covering it up.

To remove the background, make sure your image is selected and click 'remove background' from the format ribbon.

This will highlight all the bits PowerPoint is going to remove from the image in dark purple. You will also notice a box surrounding the area.

Resize this box by clicking and dragging the resize handles until the box surrounds the area of the image you want to keep as shown above. In this case, around the earth.

Once you have done this click 'keep changes'.

Notice you can now see the slide background instead of the black background on the image.

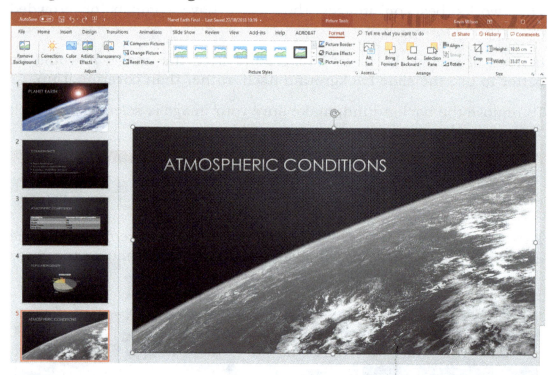

If your image is a bit more complex and doesn't have a solid background, such as this one of the shuttle, we'll need to tweak the purple mask a bit. After we align the mask box around the shuttle, if you look closely, you'll see that the purple mask has spilled over onto the edges of the wings.

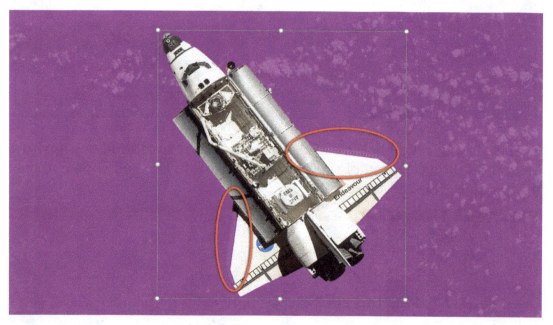

You can mark these areas of the image you don't want PowerPoint to mask out. To do this, click 'mask areas to keep'.

On your image, draw a line across the bit of the image you want to keep. In this case, the edges of the wings. Shown below.

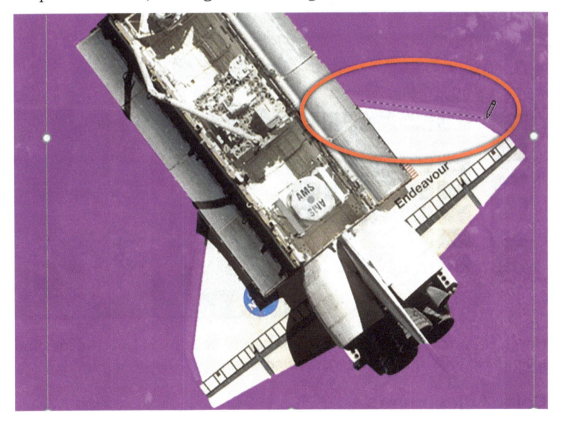

Once you've done that, you'll see the purple mask disappear from the edges of the wings.

Remember, anything highlighted in purple will be removed.

Click 'keep changes', when you're finished.

Image Effects

Image effects are features that allow you to manipulate and enhance images to improve your presentations' visual appeal or convey your message more effectively.

Corrections

Brightness and Contrast Adjustments allow you to make your images brighter or darker and adjust the contrast to make the details more pronounced or subtle. Sharpen and Soften allow you to make an image clearer or blurrier, which can be useful for focusing attention or creating a background.

Select the image on your slide. Go to the "Picture Format" tab in the Ribbon, click on "Corrections" in the Adjust group.

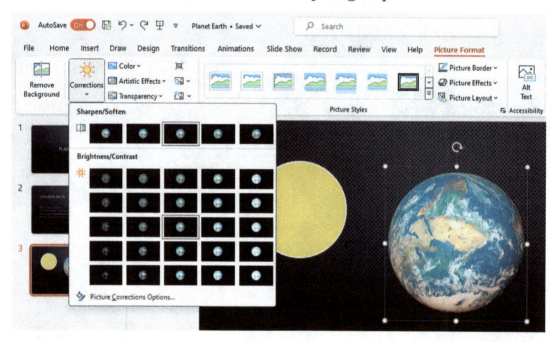

Hover over the options to preview and click to select the desired brightness, contrast, or sharpness setting.

Color Adjustments

Recolor changes the color tone of an image. This can be used to match your company's color scheme or to convey a mood (e.g., sepia for nostalgia). Saturation and Color Tone adjusts the saturation changes the intensity of the colors, while the color tone can warm up or cool down the image.

Select your image. In the "Picture Format" ribbon tab, click on "Color" in the Adjust group.

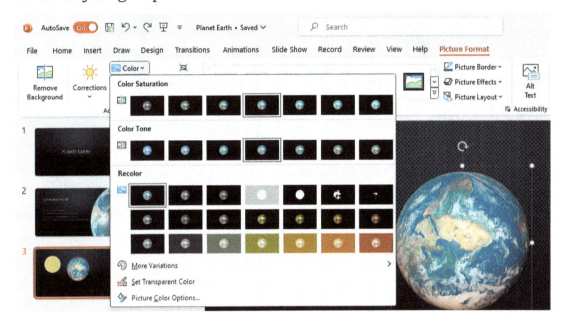

Choose from the preset color saturations, color tones, or recolor options. For more detailed adjustments, select "More Variations" or "Picture Color Options."

Artistic Effects

Filters transform your images to look like paintings, sketches, mosaics, and more. Artistic effects are great for creating themed presentations or for making stock photos more unique. Watercolor, Oil Painting, and Pencil Sketch are specific styles that mimic traditional artistic techniques.

Click on the image. In the "Picture Format" ribbon tab, find the "Artistic Effects" in the Adjust group.

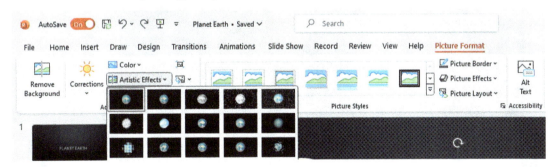

Click on "Artistic Effects" to see a dropdown menu of effects. Hover over an effect to preview it on your image, and click to apply.

Chapter 4: Adding Graphics

Picture Styles

Picture Borders add colored borders around your images. You can adjust the thickness and color of the borders to suit your design. Reflections and Shadows effects can give your images a 3D look, making them pop out of the slide. You can adjust the depth and blur of the shadow and reflection. Rounded Corners soften the appearance of your images by rounding their corners.

Select the image. In the "Picture Format" ribbon tab, select a style from the "picture styles" group.

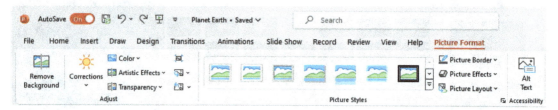

Borders

Picture borders add a frame around your images. You can customize the color, width, and style of these borders to complement your slide design. To do this, click on the image you wish to add a border to. Go to the "Picture Format" tab and click on "Picture Border" in the Picture Styles group.

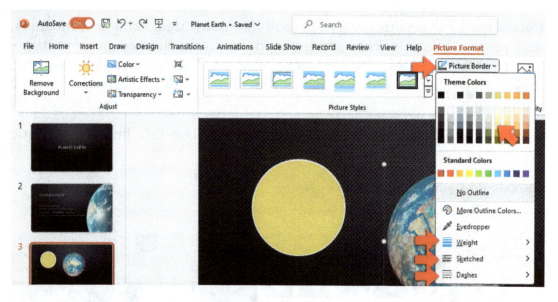

Here, you can choose the color of the border. You can further customize the border by choosing "Weight" to make the border thicker or thinner and "Dashes" to select a dashed or dotted line style instead of a solid line.

Effects

Picture effects include shadows, reflections, glow, soft edges, bevel, and 3D rotation effects. These effects can add depth, emphasis, and sophistication to your images.

Click on the image to which you want to apply effects. From the "Picture Format" ribbon tab, select "Picture Effects"

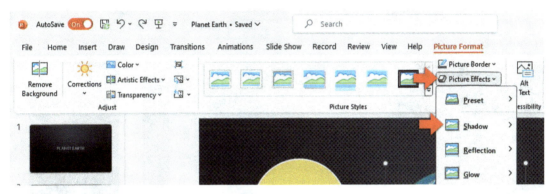

Hover over any of the effect categories to see a submenu of specific styles and options for that effect. For example, under "Shadow," you can choose from options like "Offset Bottom," "Offset Right," etc., each providing a preview as you hover over them. Click on the effect you wish to apply.

Transparency

Adjusting the transparency of images and shapes in PowerPoint allows you to create layered designs where background content can be seen through the foreground content. This is particularly useful for overlaying text on images, creating background effects, or softening elements to reduce their visual impact.

Click on the image to which you want to apply effects. From the "Picture Format" ribbon tab, select "Transparency"

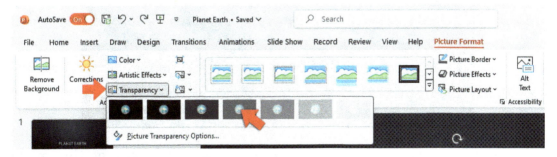

Select the from the transparencies in the drop down menu.

Design Ideas

This is a handy new feature, and appears whenever you insert an image into your slide. PowerPoint will generate some ideas on how to arrange the image you have just inserted into your slide. If you see a design you like, just click on the thumbnail, listed down the right hand side.

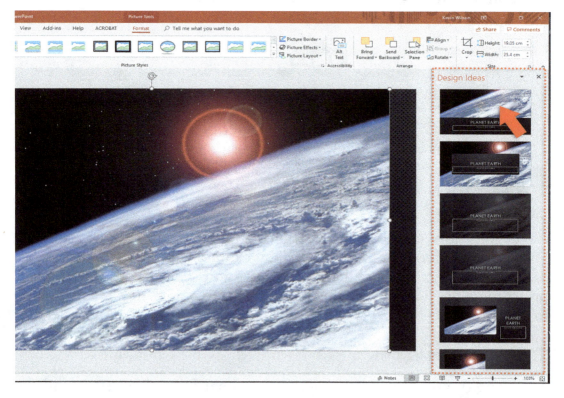

This is a quick way to format and arrange images on your slides.

If you don't choose any of the design ideas, you can arrange the image on the slide yourself.

Adding Objects

PowerPoint has a large library of objects you can add to your slides. There are speech bubbles, circles, squares, lines, arrows, stars and a whole lot more to choose from.

Shapes

To insert shapes, go to your insert ribbon and click 'shapes'. From the drop down menu you'll see a whole variety of shapes you can insert.

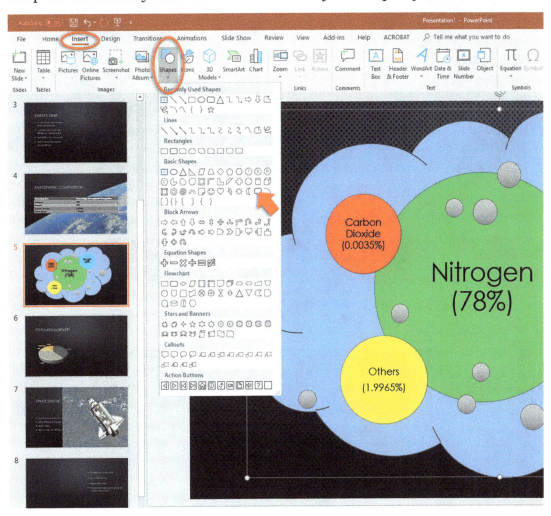

For this example, I am going to add a cloud shape to the atmosphere slide in my presentation. A cloud could represent the air, as this slide is illustrating. Inside the cloud or the air we could show the different gases.

So use the shapes to compliment and illustrate your slides.

You can change the fill color of the shape and the outline. To change the fill color, click on the shape and select your format ribbon. Click 'shape fill' and from the drop down, select a color.

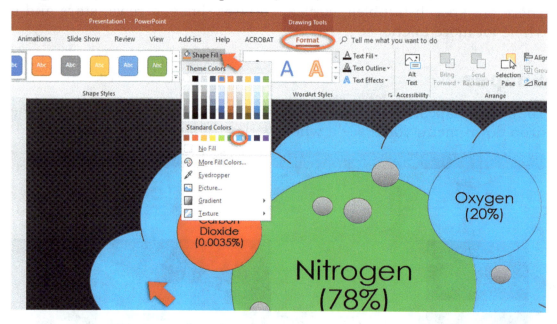

You can change the border of your shape in a similar fashion. Click your shape and from the format ribbon, select 'shape outline'.

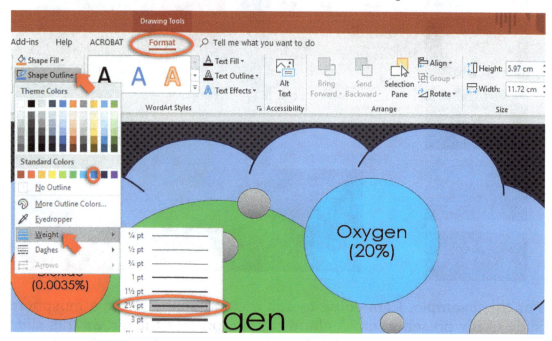

From the drop down, select a color. Then go further down the menu and select 'weight'. This is the thickness of the border. From the slide out select a border thickness.

Grouping Objects

Grouping allows you to combine multiple objects into a single unit. This is incredibly useful for moving, resizing, or applying uniform formatting to multiple elements at once without affecting their individual properties or alignment relative to one another.

Click on an object, then hold down the control key (CTRL) and click on other objects you want to group together.

Right-click one of the selected objects, go down to "Group" in the context menu. Select "Group" from the slideout menu.

To ungroup the objects, right-click on the group, go down to "Group" in the context menu. Select "ungroup" from the slideout menu.

Icons

Icons make nice little decorations and illustrations for your slides. You can use them as logos, or to illustrate a point.

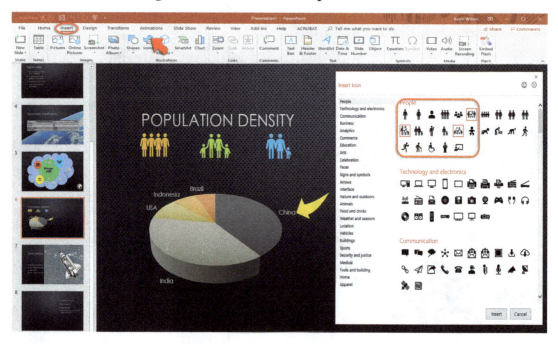

Here I'm using an arrow to point to China for having the largest population, and adding some icons of people to illustrate population.

You can change the colors of your icons. To do this, click on an icon on your slide, then from the format ribbon, select 'graphics fill'.

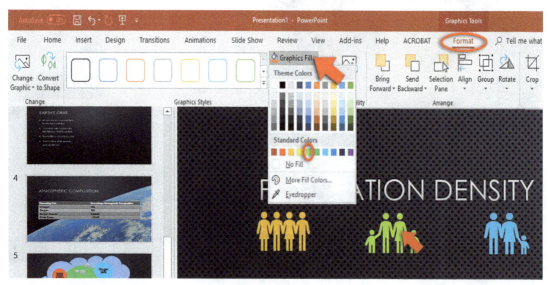

Select a color from the drop down menu.

SmartArt

SmartArt allows you to create info graphics, charts and so on. There are a lot of different types of pre-designed templates to choose from.

First, insert a new slide, or select the slide you want the SmartArt to appear. To insert SmartArt, go to your insert ribbon and click 'SmartArt'.

From the dialog box that appears, select a design. In this example, I am trying to illustrate the composition of gasses in the atmosphere, so I'm going to choose the circle design below that looks like gas molecules.

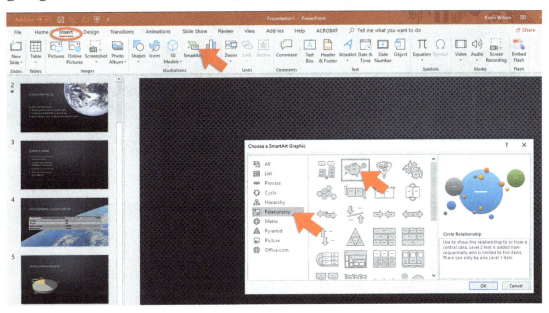

To edit the information, click in the text fields and enter your own data.

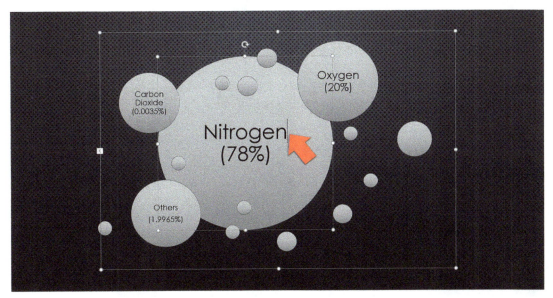

You can also change the design of the graphic. For example, change the layout, color, add some shadows?

Lets change the color of the 'other gasses' circle. To do this, click on the circle

Select the format ribbon under 'smartart tools'.

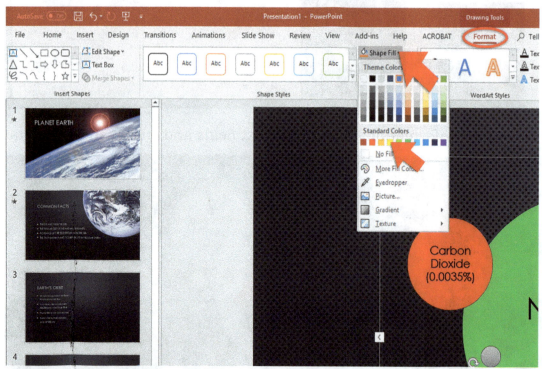

From the format ribbon, click 'shape fill'. Select a color from the drop down menu. I'm going to color this one yellow.

Try changing the colors of the other circles.

How about some shadows to separate the circles from each other and add a bit of depth to the graphic.

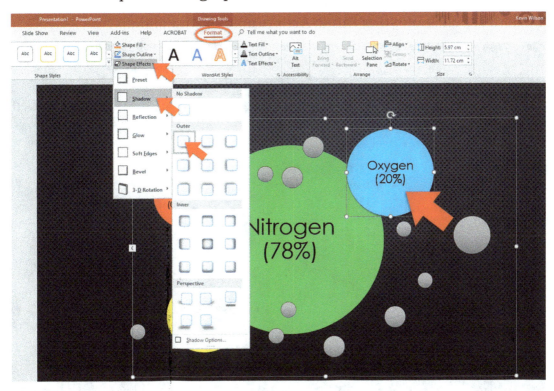

Do the same on some of the other circles. Try some of the other effects too. What about a glow?

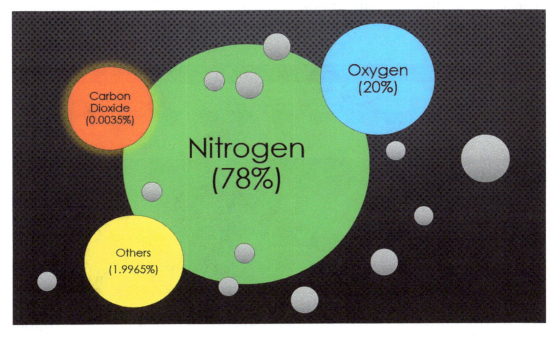

Experiment with some of the other options....

There are also some pre set styles that you can use to format your SmartArt graphic.

To do this, click on your SmartArt graphic on the slide.

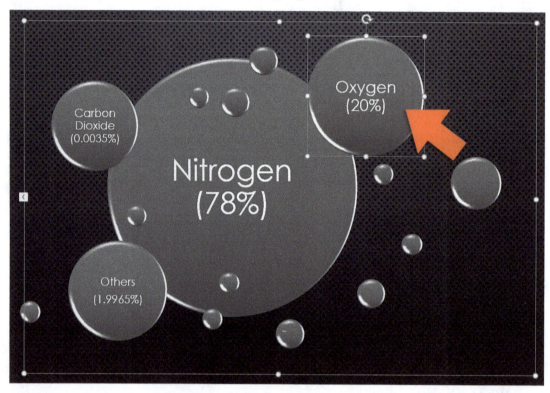

Select the 'design' ribbon under 'SmartArt tools. In the centre of your ribbon, you'll see some styles. Click on one of the icons to select the style.

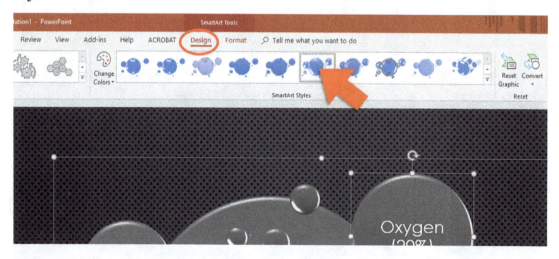

Try different ones to see what effect they have on the SmartArt graphic on your slide.

WordArt

WordArt is useful for creating headings and titles. To add wordart, select your 'insert' ribbon tab and click the wordart icon. Select a style from the drop down menu.

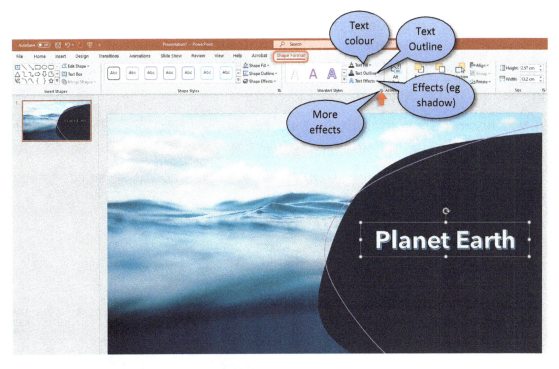

From the 'shape format' ribbon tab you can format your wordart text. To do this, use the 'wordart styles' section.

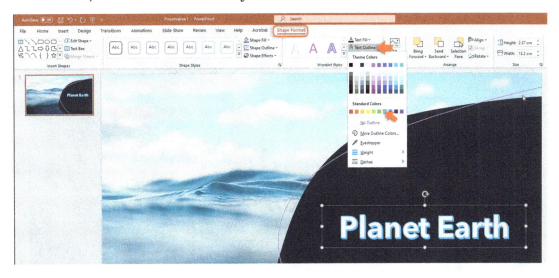

Here you can customise your text. You can change the text color, add an outline or add some effects such as shadows, reflections or a glow.

Using 3D Models

Using 3D models in PowerPoint presentations is a dynamic way to add visual interest and convey information in a more engaging and interactive manner. 3D models can be rotated and viewed from different angles, providing a comprehensive understanding of the subject matter. This feature is particularly useful for educational, technical, and design presentations where spatial understanding is crucial.

To insert a 3D model, go to the "Insert" ribbon tab, click on "3D Models" in the Illustrations group.

If you have a 3D model file on your computer (.fbx, .obj, .3mf, .ply, .stl etc), select "this device" then select the file.

In this example, I'm going to insert a stock 3D model, so select "stock 3D model" from the drop down menu.

Choose a category, select a model, and then click "Insert." You can also search for a model using the search field at the top of the dialog box.

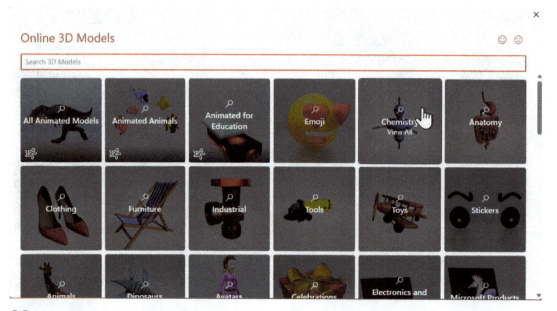

Here, I've searched for a laptop computer. Click on the model you want, then click "insert".

Once the model has been inserted, you can move and rotate it. To do this click and drag the 3D handle in the middle of the model.

Click and drag up, down, left or right to rotate the model in 3D space. This will allow you to position the model anyway you want.

Adding Animation to 3D Models

PowerPoint allows you to add animation to 3D models, making your presentations even more dynamic.

To do this, with the 3D model selected, click on the "animations" ribbon tab.

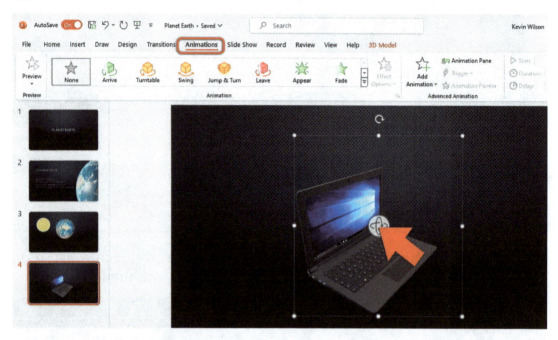

Choose an animation from the gallery. There are specific animations for 3D models, such as "Turntable," "Swing," and "Jump & Turn," which animate the model rotating or moving in space.

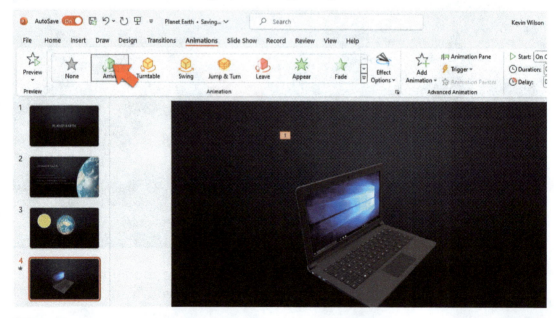

Custom Shapes & Freeform Drawing

Custom shapes and freeform drawing allow you to create unique graphics and illustrations that go beyond the pre-defined shape library. These tools are useful for designing specific visuals that match your content's needs, from highlighting parts of an image to crafting entirely new shapes for your presentation.

Combine Shapes

Insert two or more shapes onto your slide. Select the shapes - hold down the "CTRL" key and click on each shape.

Go to the "Shape Format" ribbon tab, and find the "Merge Shapes" dropdown in the "Insert Shapes" group. Choose from the options like "Union," "Combine," "Fragment," "Intersect," and "Subtract" to create a new custom shape based on how you want to merge the selected shapes

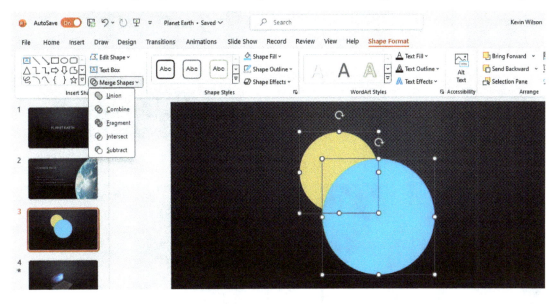

Lets try "subtract".

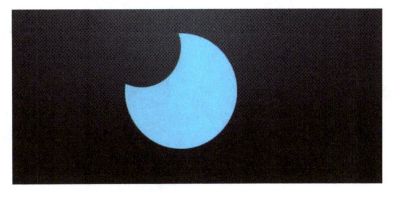

Freeform Drawing

The Freeform tool lets you draw shapes with your mouse, touchpad, or touch screen, providing the freedom to create virtually any shape you can imagine.

To do this, go to the "Insert" ribbon tab, click on "Shapes" and choose the "Scribble" tool under the "Lines" group.

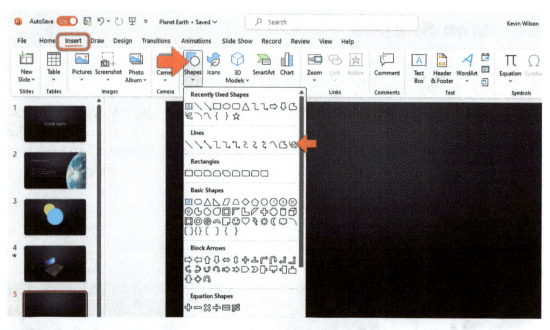

Draw the shape you want, and release the mouse button to finish.

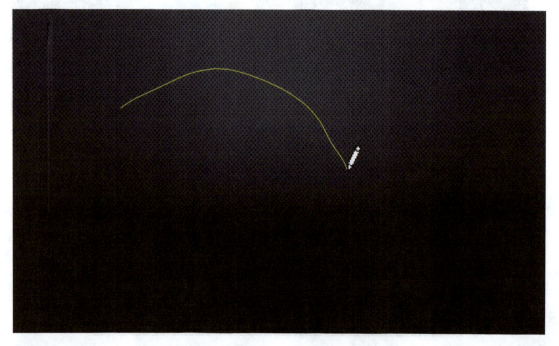

Sometimes the drawing will appear as black. To change the color, with the drawing selected, from the "shape format" ribbon tab, select "shape outline". Select a color from the pallet. To change the size, go down to "weight", select a thickness from the slideout menu.

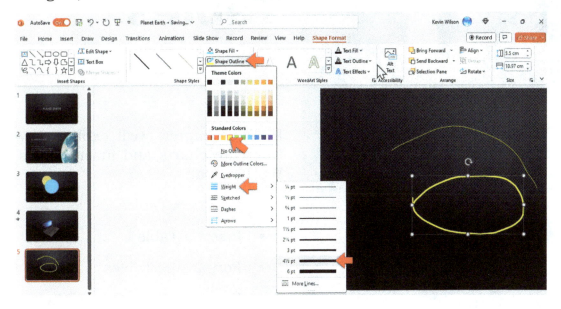

Pen Support

In Microsoft PowerPoint, you'll see an additional ribbon tab called 'draw'. This has all your drawing tools such as pens, highlighters and an eraser for you to annotate your presentations.

Select the 'draw' ribbon tab and select a pen color from the selections in the centre of the ribbon. From here you can select the color and thickness of your pen.

You can annotate and draw on your slides in preparation for your presentation and when you save your presentation, PowerPoint will save your drawings and annotations as well.

If you're presenting live, you can use the pen tools in Slide Show view to dynamically interact with your slides.

5

Charts & Tables

In this chapter, we'll explore how to create charts and insert tables. We'll look at:

- Charts & Tables
- Insert a Table
- Formatting Tables
- Inserting Excel Spreadsheets
- Add a Chart
- Formatting Charts

To help you better understand this section, take a look at the video resources. Open your web browser and navigate to the following website:

elluminetpress.com/ppt-grap

You'll also need to download the source files from:

elluminetpress.com/ppt

Insert a Table

We are going to add a table to a new slide. In this example I have added a new slide with 'title and content'. You can also add a table from the insert ribbon.

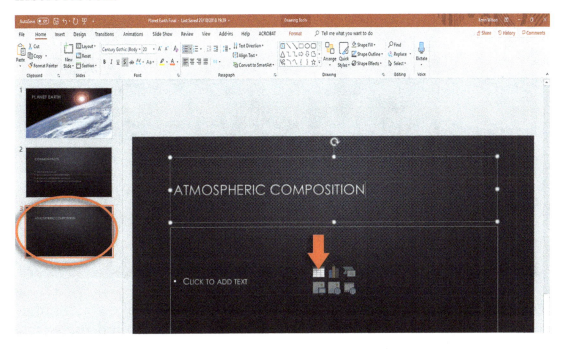

To add a table to this slide, just click the table icon from the template as indicated above. In the dialog box that appears, enter the number of columns and rows. This table is going to have 2 columns.

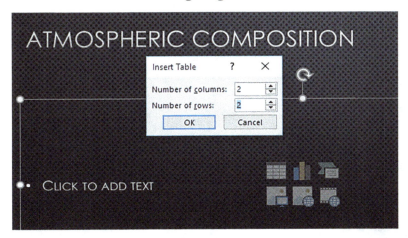

Once you have done that, enter the data into your table. Press the tab key to move between cells of the table. Don't worry about the number of rows, a new row will be inserted at the end of each row when entering your data - just press tab.

You can also insert a table directly. To do this, go to your insert ribbon and click 'table'.

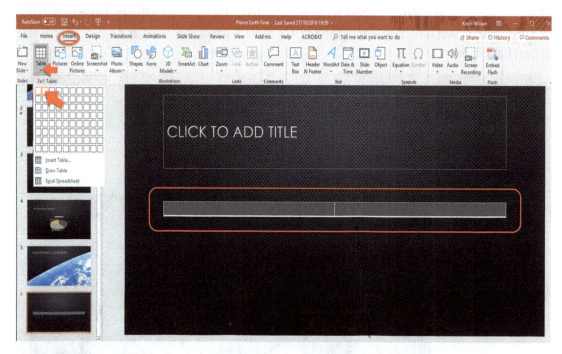

You can move or resize the table. If you click on the table, you'll notice an outline appear around the table with small dots around the edges. These are called resize handles and you can click and drag them to resize your table.

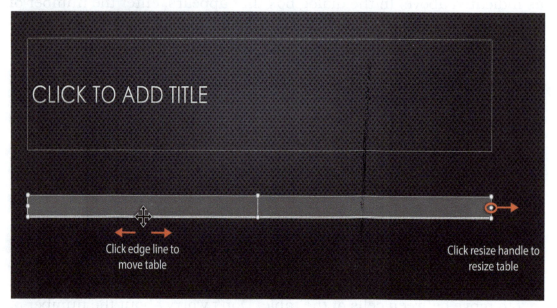

If you click on the edge line of the table and drag your mouse, you can move your table to the desired position on your slide.

Formatting Tables

To do basic formatting, select the table with your mouse and click your design ribbon.

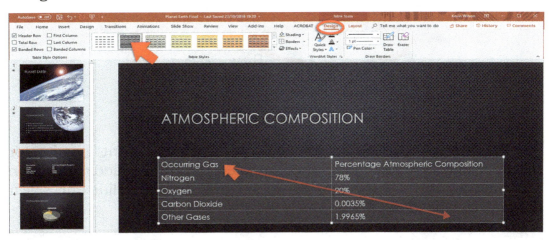

From here you can add some borders, change the shading or add an effect.

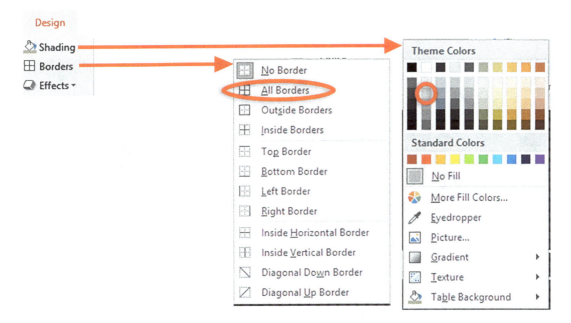

Click 'shading' and add a background color to the cells. Since the slide is mostly grey, I'm going to choose a lighter grey to compliment the slide color.

Then click borders, and select 'all borders' to put a border around all cells. You can also select individual cells or groups of cells and add borders to those to emphasise different parts of the table.

Chapter 5: Charts & Tables

You can adjust the border thickness using the 'draw borders' section of the design ribbon. Click the drop down circled below and from the menu, select a thickness.

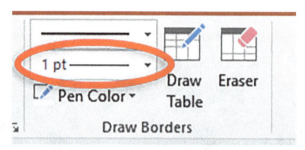

Finally click 'effects'. Select the type of effect you want (shadow or reflection effects work well). In the example, I am going to add a reflection effect to the table. Go down to 'reflection' and from the slide out, select the type of reflection effect.

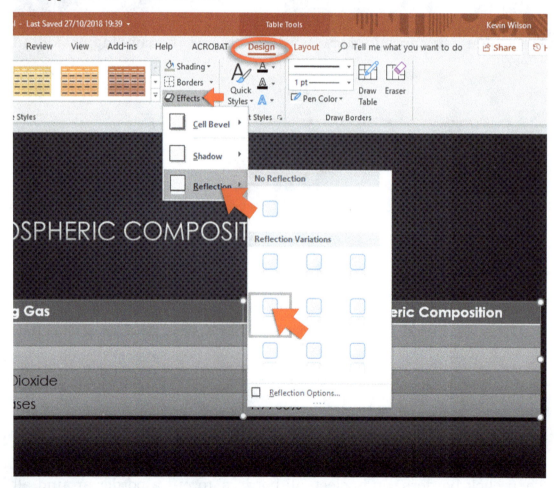

Try experiment with some of the other borders, shadings and effects using these controls.

Table Themes

You can format your table using PowerPoint's pre-designed themes. This makes formatting your table quick and easy.

Click on the table then select the Design ribbon.

Along the centre of the Design ribbon you will see a number of pre sets. Click the small down arrow at the bottom right to expand the selections, circled above.

Click on a design to apply it to the table.

You can experiment with the designs by clicking on these and see how they look.

PowerPoint will automatically format the table using the colors and shadings in the themes.

Inserting Excel Spreadsheets

Inserting Excel spreadsheets into PowerPoint presentations is a handy technique that allows you to display Excel data directly within a PowerPoint slide.

You can link a spreadsheet or embed it into the slide. Embedding the spreadsheet, involves inserting a copy directly onto the slide making it self-contained, eliminating the need for external files. However, e the embedded spreadsheet does not update automatically with changes made to the source file, it can quickly become outdated unless manually updated.

Linking creates a dynamic connection to the spreadsheet file, meaning the content automatically updates to reflect changes in the source spreadsheet file. This ensures that your linked spreadsheet always displays the most current data. The downside, however, is that the linked spreadsheet depends on the external spreadsheet file. If the this file is moved, renamed, or deleted, the link breaks, leading to incorrect or missing data.

To insert a spreadsheet, open your PowerPoint Presentation, navigate to the slide where you want to embed the Excel spreadsheet. Go to the "Insert" ribbon tab, then click on "Object" in the "Text" group.

Click 'create from file' on the left hand side of the dialog box.

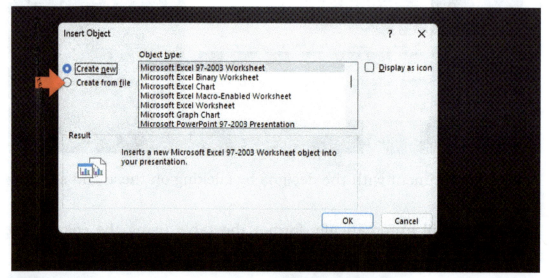

Click on "Browse" to navigate to the location of the Excel file you want to insert.

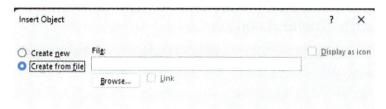

Select the spreadsheet you want to insert. Click "ok".

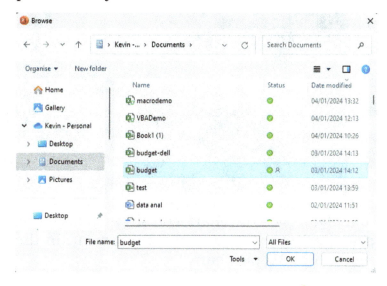

If you want the data in the PowerPoint slide to update automatically whenever changes are made to the original Excel file, check the "Link" checkbox. Click "ok".

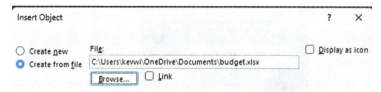

Once the spreadsheet has been inserted, go to the "shape format" ribbon. Here you can change the border and fill color.

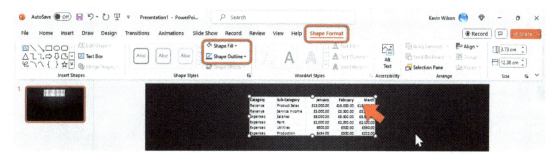

Add a Chart

We are going to add a chart to a new slide. In this example I have added a new slide with 'title and content'

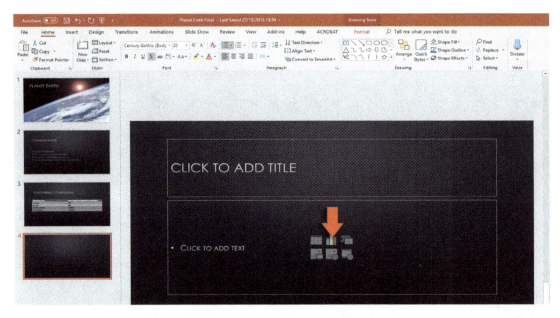

On the slide template, click the chart icon shown above. From the dialog box that appears, select the type of chart you want. In this example, I am going to use a nice 3D pie chart.

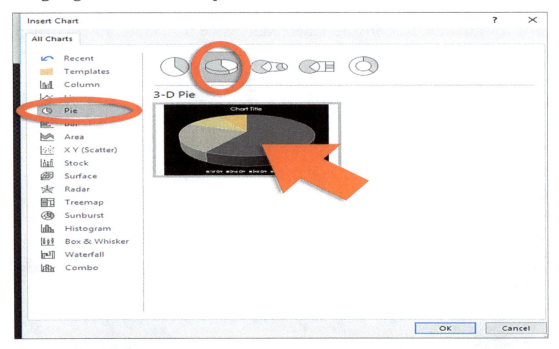

Click OK when you are done.

You'll see a spreadsheet like table open up where you can add some data. Enter the data in table shown below.

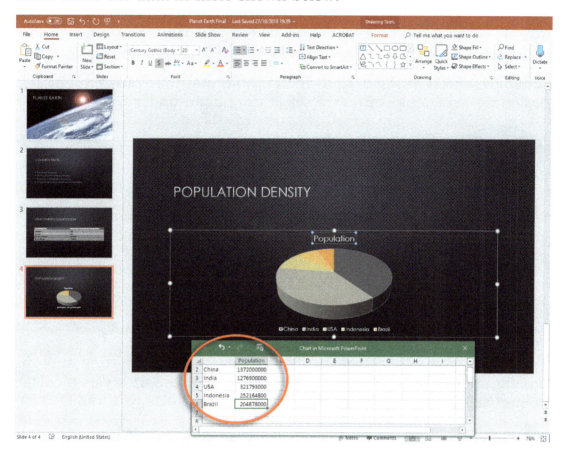

As you enter your data, you'll notice PowerPoint begins to construct your chart.

Remember when constructing your charts, **Column A** is the **X axis** on your chart, **Column B** is the **Y axis**.

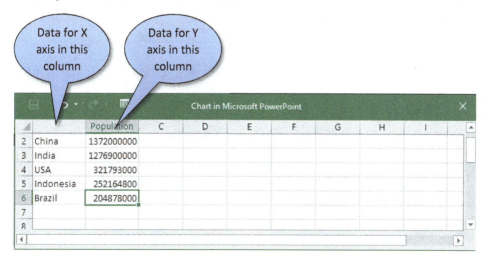

Formatting Charts

PowerPoint has a few chart formatting tools to take note of. First click on your chart to select it, you'll notice two new ribbons appear: design and format.

Lets have a look at the design ribbon. Note that there are actually two design ribbons. Make sure you select the ribbon under 'chart tools'.

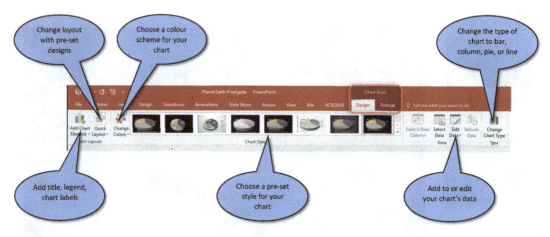

From here, you can do most of your basic chart formatting such as adding titles, editing your chart data and apply chart styles to make your charts look more visually appealing.

Chart Titles

To a chart title, click on your chart and select the design ribbon. From the design ribbon, click 'add chart element'. Go down to 'chart title' and from the slide out click 'above chart'.

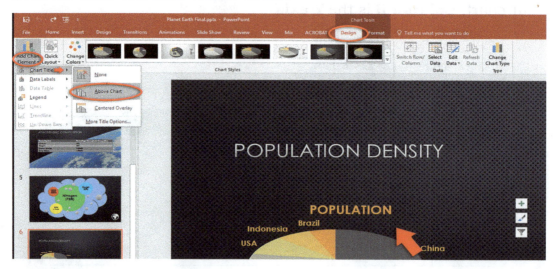

Data Labels

Data labels are the labels that describe what the elements of the chart represent. You can either label each element of the chart or use a chart legend.

Click on your chart.

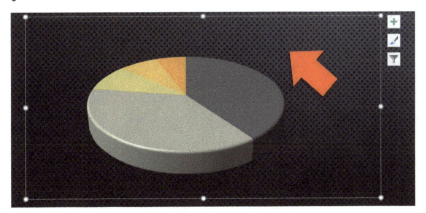

Select 'add chart element' from the design ribbon. From the drop down menu, go down to 'data labels' and from the slide out, click 'data callout' or 'outside end'.

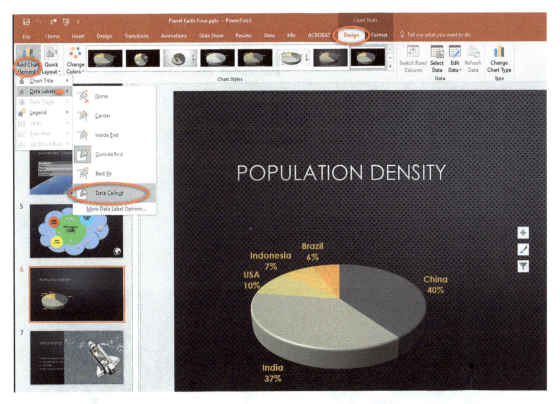

This tells PowerPoint where to position your labels.

Chart Legends

Chart legends are good for explaining what the different parts of your chart represent.

To add a legend to your chart, click on your chart and select your design ribbon, then click 'add chart element'.

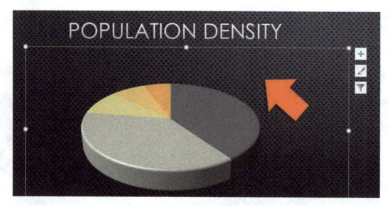

From the drop down menu, go down to 'legend' and from the slide out, click on the position you want the legend.

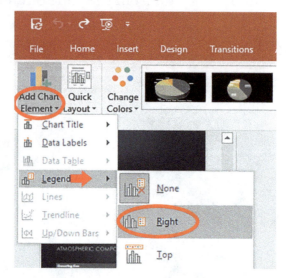

On the right is usually a good place.

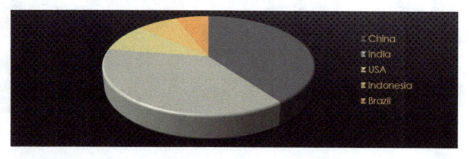

Edit Chart Data

To edit your chart data, click on your chart to select it.

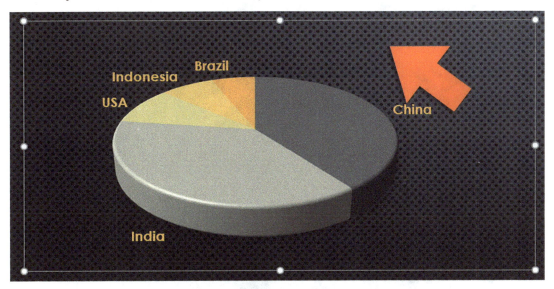

Select your design ribbon under 'chart tools'. Click on 'edit data'. If you get a drop down menu, select 'edit data' again.

You'll see a spreadsheet like window open up with the data used to generate your chart.

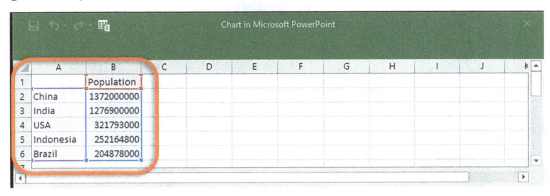

You can edit the data or add to the data from here and PowerPoint will automatically update your chart accordingly.

Chart Styles

You can style your charts pretty quickly using the style options on your design ribbon.

First, click your chart to select it.

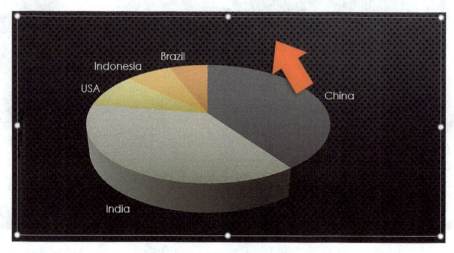

Go to the 'design' ribbon under 'chart tools'. On the centre of your design ribbon, you'll see some chart styles. Click on one of the thumbnail icons to apply a style to your chart.

PowerPoint will apply the style to your chart.

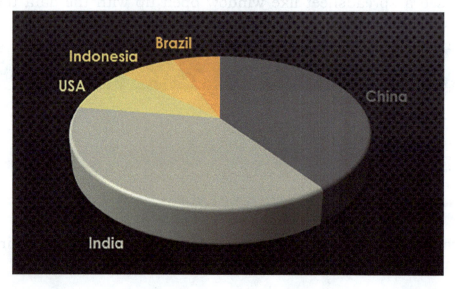

Chart Color Schemes

You can also change the color schemes (the colors used to represent the different data in your chart).

Sometimes the colors aren't as clear, so having the ability to choose different color schemes helps with clarity and makes your chart stand out a bit more on your slide.

To do this, click on your chart to select it.

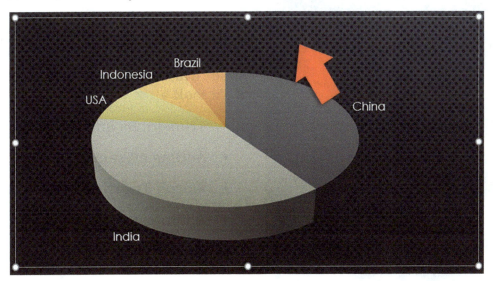

From the design ribbon under 'chart tools', click 'change colors'.

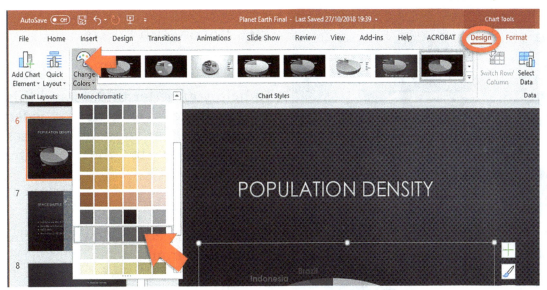

From the drop down menu, select a color scheme that shows up your chart clearly and matches the colors of your slide.

6

Transitions and Animations

In this chapter, we'll explore how bring your presentation to life with slide transitions and animations. We'll look at:

- Transitions and Animations
- Adding a Transition
- Morph Transitions
- Adding an Animation
- Customize the Animation
- Motion Paths
- Custom Motion Paths
- Motion Path Effects
- Timing and Order

To help you better understand this section, take a look at the video resources. Open your web browser and navigate to the following website:

elluminetpress.com/ppt-tns

You'll also need to download the source files from:

elluminetpress.com/ppt

Slide Transitions

Slide transitions in PowerPoint refer to the animation effects applied to the movement from one slide to another during a presentation. These transitions add visual interest and can help to maintain audience engagement by creating smooth and dynamic shifts between slides.

Types

There are various types of transitions to choose from, ranging from subtle fades to more elaborate animations. Some common types of transitions include:

- **Fade:** The current slide gradually fades out while the next slide fades in. It provides a smooth and subtle transition between slides.

- **Push:** The current slide is pushed aside to reveal the next slide. This transition creates a dynamic effect as the new slide appears to "push" the previous one off-screen.

- **Wipe:** The next slide "wipes" over the current slide from a specified direction, such as left to right or top to bottom. It gives the impression of one slide replacing another in a clean, horizontal or vertical motion.

- **Zoom:** The next slide zooms in from a specified point, gradually filling the screen. This transition can add a dramatic effect by emphasizing specific elements or details on the new slide.

- **Dissolve:** The current slide dissolves into the next slide, gradually fading away to reveal the new content. It provides a gentle and seamless transition between slides.

- **Checkerboard:** The screen is divided into a grid of squares, which flip to reveal the next slide underneath. .

- **Cube:** The current slide rotates like a cube to reveal the next slide on a different face of the cube. It adds a three-dimensional effect to the transition between slides, creating a sense of depth and movement.

While transitions can add visual interest, it's essential to use them judiciously. A subtle transitions like "Fade" is often more professional and less distracting compared to a flashy one like "Cube". Also using different transitions on each slide can be jarring and disrupt the flow of the presentation. Consistency creates a cohesive look and ensures that the audience focuses on the content rather than the effects.

Adding a Transition

To add transitions to PowerPoint slides, click the slide you want to add the transition to, then go to the transitions ribbon.

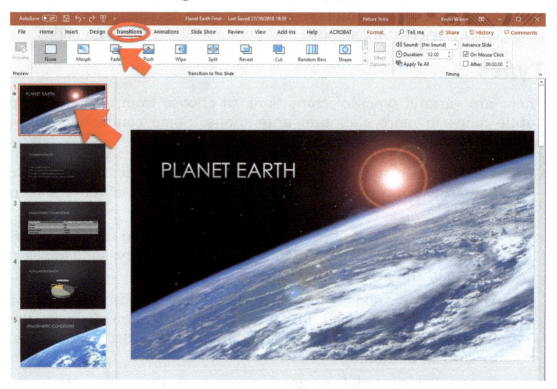

From the transitions ribbon, you can select from several pre set transitions. If you click on a transition, for example 'fade', this will apply the transition to the selected slide.

You can change the duration of the transition. The current duration is 0.7 seconds. If you want a slower transition, increase the duration. Try 1 or 2 seconds.

You can tell PowerPoint to wait for a mouse click to transition to the next slide, or you can make PowerPoint transition to the next slide after a set time. On the far right of your transitions ribbon, use 'on mouse click' to transition to next slide when you click the mouse, or un-check 'on mouse click' box and adjust the timer where it says 'after' with the length of time to display the slide.

To apply the transition to the whole presentation, click 'apply to all' on the right hand side of the ribbon.

Morph Transitions

The morph transition allows you to animate objects from one slide to the other. You can use text, shapes, pictures, charts, WordArt, and SmartArt.

To use the morph transition, you'll need two slides with at least one object appearing on both. The best way to achieve this is to create one slide with all the objects in the start position, then duplicate the slide and move the objects into the finish position. First slide morphs into second slide.

Create a new slide. In this example, I'm going to add the three planets, venus, earth and mars. This is the slide with all the objects in the start position of the morph animation.

Now, duplicate the slide. This slide has all the objects in the end position.

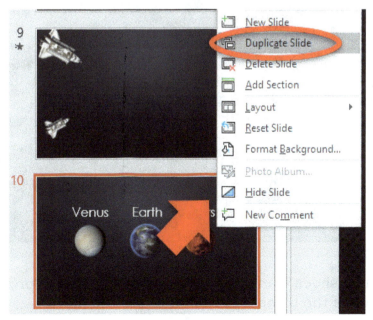

On the duplicate slide, move and resize the objects into the end position. You can also add more objects. I'm going to add a text box to show the stats for planet earth

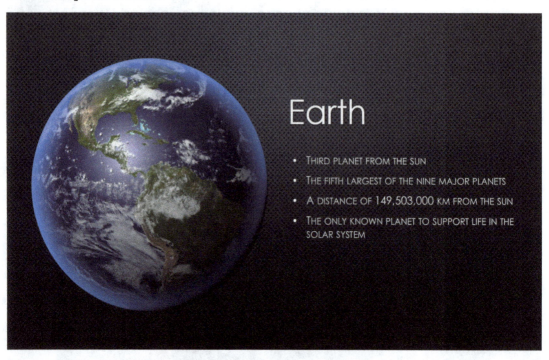

On the transitions ribbon, select morph.

Watch the two slides transition into each other. Click 'preview' on the left hand side of the transition ribbon to see the morph.

Animations

Animations allow you to bring objects on your slides to life, adding movement and interactivity to your presentations.

Types

There are various different types of animations depending on what you want to do with the object. You can add animations to move text boxes, make bullet points appear, animate shapes and so on. This can help to make your presentation flow so objects and text appear at the right time while you're presenting. Animation effects can also help to emphasise certain points. Let's take a look at some of the most common animations.

Entrance Animations animations bring elements onto the slide, such as text or images, when they are first introduced.

- **Appear:** Object gradually appears on the slide.
- **Fade In:** Object fades into view from transparent to opaque.
- **Fly In:** Object flies onto the slide from a specified direction.
- **Zoom In:** Object zooms into view, gradually increasing in size.

Exit Animations remove elements from the slide, making them disappear when no longer needed.

- **Fade Out:** Object fades out of view from opaque to transparent.
- **Fly Out:** Object flies off the slide in a specified direction.
- **Zoom Out:** Object zooms out of view, gradually decreasing in size.
- **Collapse:** Object collapses and disappears from view.

Emphasis Animations highlight or draw attention to specific elements already on the slide, such as making text bold or enlarging an image.

- **Grow & Shrink:** Object alternates between growing and shrinking in size.
- **Spin:** Object spins in place, rotating around its center.
- **Pulse:** Object pulsates or throbs in size, appearing to expand and contract.
- **Color Emphasis:** Object changes color to draw attention.

Motion Path Animations allow you to move elements along a specified path on the slide, such as a curve or a straight line.

Action Animations trigger an animation when a specific action occurs, such as clicking on a button or hovering over an object.

Adding an Animation

Looking at the slide below, lets say you wanted each bullet point to appear one at a time, instead of all at once.

To do this, we can add an entrance animation to the text box. First click on the text box, then select your animations ribbon tab.

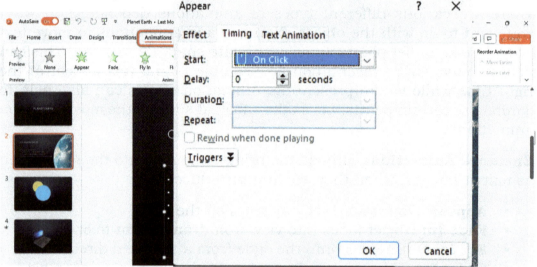

Click on 'add animation'. Here, you'll see a list of all the different types of animations you can add. For this example, I am going to add a fade effect. This is under the 'entrance effects', as we want each bullet point in this example to appear.

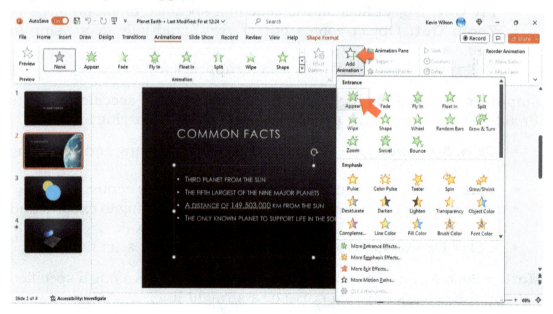

Try one of the other effects and see what happens. You can apply an effect, in the same way, to any object, photo, textbox, heading or logo

Customize the Animation

To customize the animation, click on the "Animation Pane" button in the Advanced Animation group. This will open the Animation Pane on the right side of the screen, showing a list of all animations on the slide.

In the Animation Pane, locate the animation you want to customize, such as the "Appear" animation. Double-click on the animation. This will open the "Effect Options" dialog box.

Effect Tab allows you to modify the specific effect settings for the animation. Sound allows you to select a sound to play when the animation occurs.

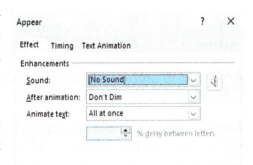

After animation allows you to choose what happens to the text or object after the animation plays.

Animate text allows you to control how the text enters or exits. For instance, you can set it to "All at once", "By word", or "By letter". There may also be a delay option, to control the time between the animations of individual words or letters.

Timing Tab enables you to control the timing and duration of the animation.

Start determines when the animation will begin eg when you click the mouse. Delay sets a delay time before the animation starts.

Duration sets how long the animation will take from start to finish. A shorter duration means a faster animation, while a longer duration makes it slower.

Repeat allows you to set how many times the animation will repeat. You can choose a specific number of times or have it repeat until another action is taken.

Text Animation Tab appears when you apply animation to text elements. Group text allows you to choose the level of text to animate in a grouped manner. "By 1st Level Paragraphs" means that each paragraph or bullet point at the first level of your text hierarchy will be

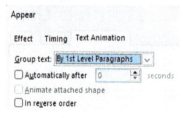

animated separately. You could also choose to animate by 2nd level paragraphs, and so on, depending on how your text is structured.

Automatically after allows you to set the animation to proceed automatically after a certain number of seconds. This can be used to automate your presentation so that it runs by itself.

Animate attached shape means that any shape that is attached to the text will also be animated along with the text.

In reverse order will animate the text in reverse order. For instance, if you have a list of bullet points, the last point will be animated first and the first point last.

Motion Paths

A motion path is an animation effect that allows you to move an object such as a photo, shape or text box across the screen.

To create a motion path, first click on the object you want to animate. For simplicity's sake, I'm going to use a circle. Go to your animations ribbon, click 'add animation' and select 'lines' from the motion path section of the drop down menu.

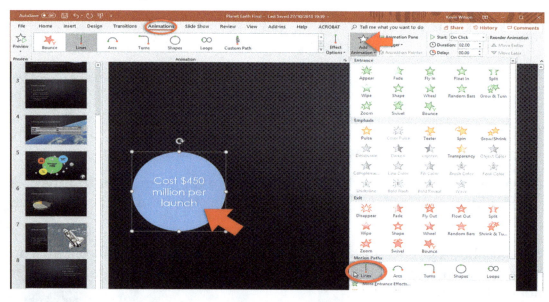

Now, if you look really closely, you'll see two very small dots on the light blue circles. One dot is green, this is the starting point. The other dot is red, this is the end point.

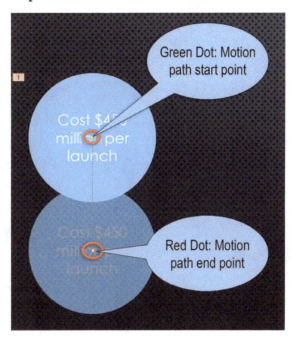

To create a motion path, you need to drag the green dot to the point you want the object to start at, then drag the red dot to the point you want the object to end up.

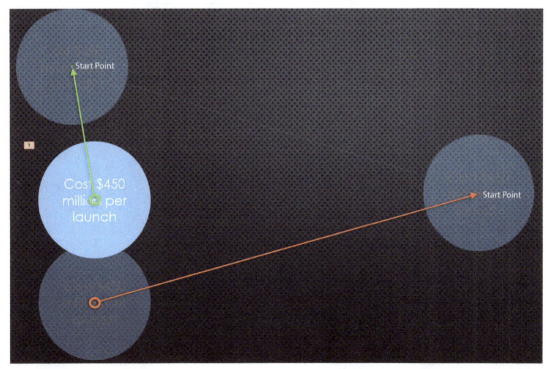

If you click 'preview' on the top left of your animations ribbon, you'll see the circle move left to right across the screen.

You can apply this effect to any object, textbox, photo or heading. You can also use different paths: arcs, turns or loops, and manipulate them in the same way, by moving the start and end points. Try an arc, to move the path, drag the resize handles on the box around the arc path.

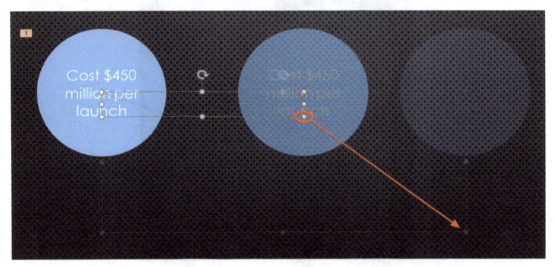

So you end up with something like this... you can see the motion path arc down then back up in a 'U' shape.

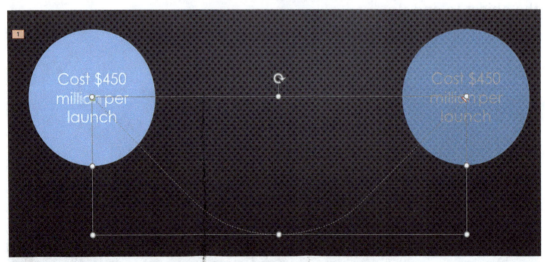

If the resize box disappears, click back on the motion path.

Custom Motion Paths

You can also draw your own paths if you prefer. Click on the object you want to animate. Go to your animations ribbon, click 'add animation'.

From the drop down menu, go right down to the bottom and click 'custom path'.

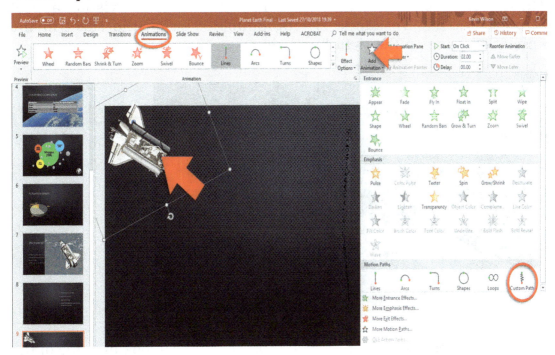

Now draw the path on the slide with your mouse. Highlighted below in red.

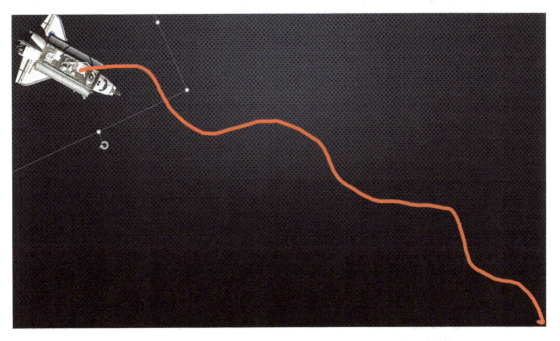

Double click on the position on the slide you want the object to end on. Now, when you preview your slide, you'll see the ship fly to the bottom right corner.

Motion Path Effects

These effects play a crucial role in enhancing the visual appeal of presentations. To adjust effects, double click on the effect in the animation pane on the right hand side.

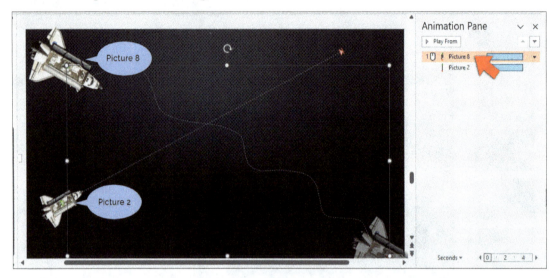

In the dialog box, select the 'effect' tab. Let's take a look at some of the effects you can add to the motion path

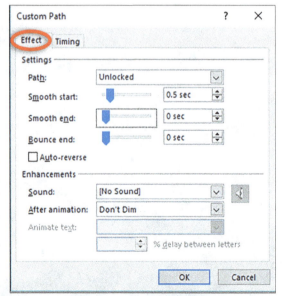

Path option would typically be active for motion path animations Locked means that the path of the motion cannot be changed. Unlocked means that you can edit the path.

Smooth start controls how smoothly an animation begins. A higher value makes the animation start more slowly and gradually speed up.

Smooth end controls how smoothly the animation concludes. Like the smooth start, a higher value here makes the animation decelerate and come to a stop more gently.

Bounce end adds a "bounce" effect at the end of the animation, where the object will move slightly past its final point and then settle back into place. You can control the extent of this bounce with the given duration.

Auto-reverse will play in reverse after completing, returning to the starting point.

Sound will play with the animation. The dropdown shows "No Sound" selected, but you can choose from available sounds.

After animation allows you to select what happens to the object after the animation plays. Options like "Don't Dim" will keep the object at full brightness, while other options may dim the object or make it disappear.

Animate text allows you to set a delay between the animation of letters, words, or sentences. The "% delay between letters" box allows you to specify the delay.

Timing and Order

Using the animation page you can adjust timings and the order of your animations. To open the pane, select the 'animations' ribbon tab, then click on 'animation pane'.

You'll see the animation pane appear on the right hand side of the screen.

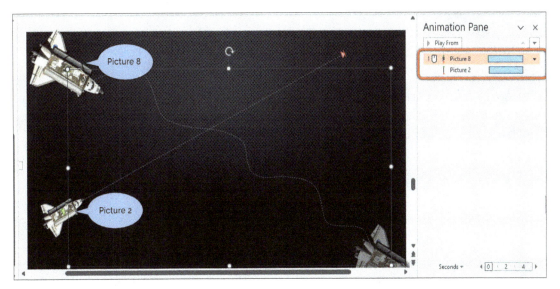

In this slide, we have two images, note their names: 'Picture 8' and 'Picture 2' as listed in the animation pane.

Next to the object names in the animation pane, you'll see a blue bar. This is a timing bar and indicates how long the animation on that particular object is.

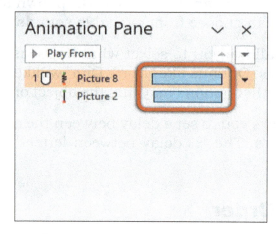

The left hand side of the bar indicates the start while the right hand side of the bar indicates the end of the animation. You'll see a meter right at the bottom of the animation pane showing the number of seconds. In the example below, the animations will last 4 seconds.

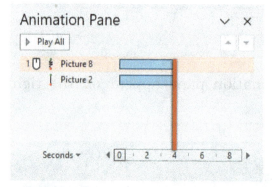

You can change the length of the animation by dragging the right hand edge line of the blue bar to the right, in the animation pane. You'll see the number of seconds on the end increase.

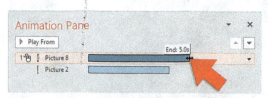

You can get the animations on the objects to start at the same time. On the animations pane, the first object in the list has a small mouse icon next to it, this means that the animation on that object will start when the user clicks the mouse.

Right click on the second object in the list and from the drop down menu, click 'start with previous'.

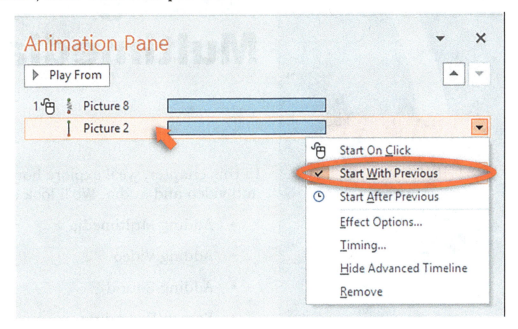

Now both animations will start at the same time. If you wanted 'picture 2' to start a bit after 'picture 8', drag the left hand edge of the blue bar next to 'picture 2', to the right. You'll see some seconds. This is the amount of time before the animation on this object starts. In this example, 'picture 2' will start 1.6 seconds after the user clicks the mouse.

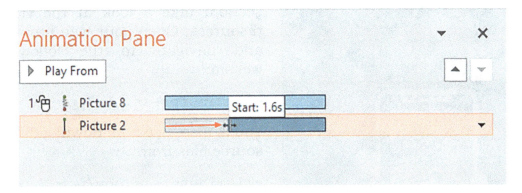

Picture 8 will start as soon as the user clicks the mouse.

This is useful if you have a sequence of objects that need to appear at different times during the slide animation.

7

Adding Multimedia

In this chapter, we'll explore how to add video and audio. We'll look at:

- Adding Multimedia
- Adding Video
- Adding Sound
- Screen Recording
- Recording Presentations
- Export your Presentation
- Photo Albums

To help you better understand this section, take a look at the video resources. Open your web browser and navigate to the following website:

elluminetpress.com/ppt-mm

You'll also need to download the source files from:

elluminetpress.com/ppt

Adding Video

You can add videos from your computer and videos from an online video sharing source such as YouTube.

Add Video on your PC to a New Slide

To add a video to a new slide, click 'new slide' from your home ribbon. From the drop down menu, click 'content with caption.

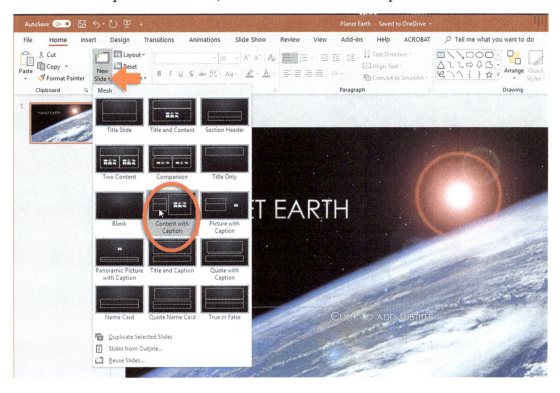

On the new slide, click the 'insert video' icon

Select 'from a file', then from the popup dialog box, navigate to the folder on your computer where your video is saved. In this example, the video is in the 'videos' folder.

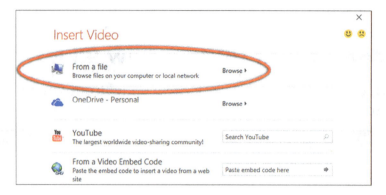

Double click on the video you want to add.

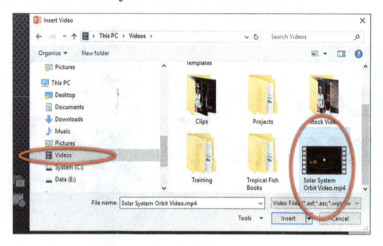

Add a title and some bullet points to your slide and here we go.

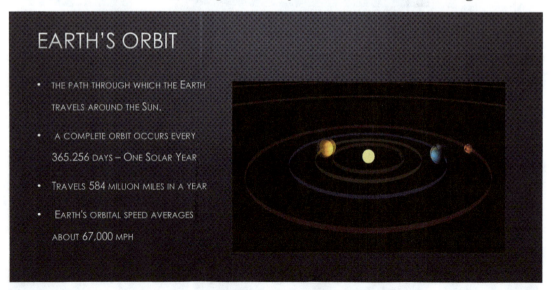

Add video from your PC to an Existing slide

If you already have a slide that you would like to add video to, go to your insert ribbon and click 'video'.

From the drop down click 'video from my pc'. Select 'online video' if you are linking to a YouTube video.

From the dialog box, double click the video you want to insert.

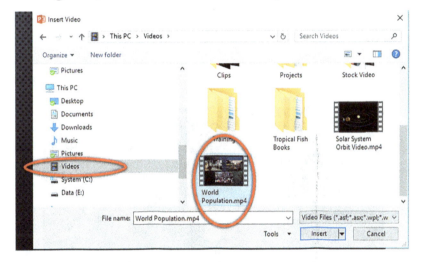

You may need to resize your video, if you don't want it to fill the screen. You can do this by clicking and dragging the resize handles on the edges of the video.

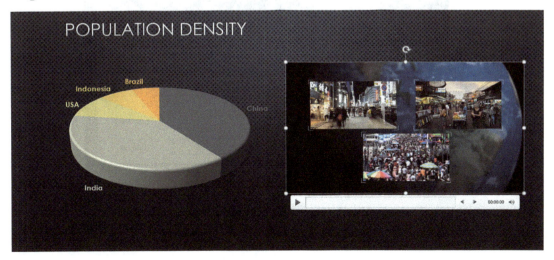

Trimming Videos

You can trim videos to start in exactly the right place. You can't do this with online videos yet, but you can trim any that have been downloaded to your computer.

Click on your video and from the playback ribbon, click 'trim video'.

From the popup dialog box, drag the start point towards the right (indicated in red, above), to the point where you want the video to start. You'll see a preview of the video at the top of the dialog box.

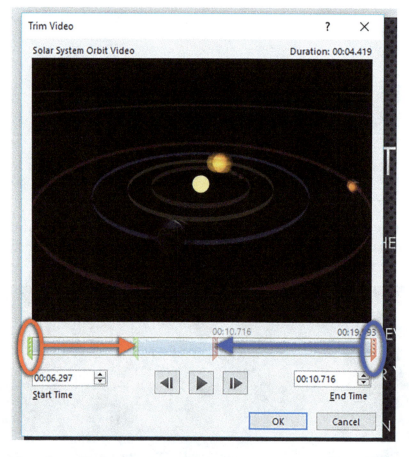

Do the same with the end point. Drag the end point to the left (indicated in blue, above), to the point you want the video to stop.

Click OK when you're done.

Online

You can link to YouTube videos from your slide. Insert a blank slide, then from your insert ribbon click 'video'. From the drop down menu select 'online video'.

From the popup dialog box, go down to YouTube, and in the search field type in what you're looking for. In this example, I'm looking for a video to go on my space shuttle page, so I typed 'space shuttle launch'.

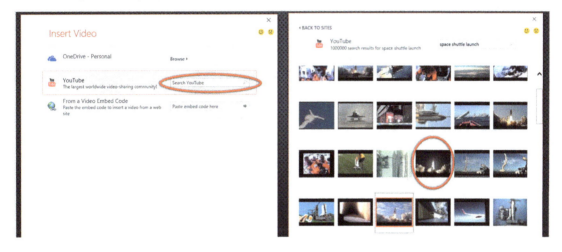

Double click on the video thumbnail in the search results to add the video to your PowerPoint slide. You might need to resize your video and move it into position on your slide. Add some information about it too.

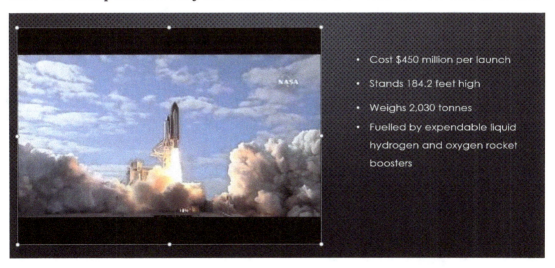

Adding Sound

You can add audio files that contain music or voice as well as record your own audio.

Recording Audio

To record audio, the first thing you should do is invest in a good microphone, especially if you intend to use your recordings as voice overs or links in a recorded presentation. This will vastly improve the quality.

The mic pictured below is a fairly inexpensive option.

This type of microphone will plug directly into a USB port on your computer or laptop with little or no configuration, which makes it ideal for PowerPoint presentations.

This comes in handy for recording narrations and presentations. We'll cover this a bit later.

Audio from your PC

If you already have a slide that you would like to add audio to, go to your insert ribbon and click 'audio'. From the drop down click 'audio on my pc'.

From the dialog box that appears, browse to the audio file you want to insert. In this example, my audio is stored in my music folder.

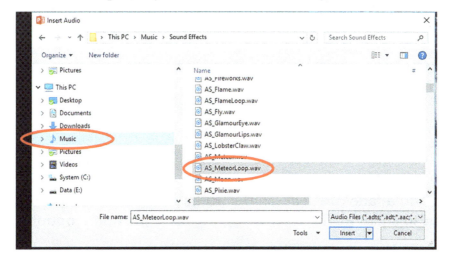

Your audio will show up as an icon on your slide.

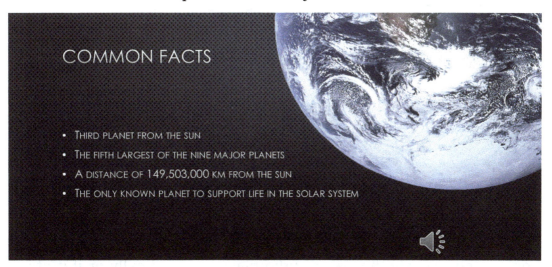

By default, you'll need to click the icon when showing your presentation to start the audio.

To change the audio settings, click on the audio icon on the slide

Select the 'playback' ribbon under 'audio tools'.

From here you can listen to a preview, trim the audio clip so it starts and ends in specific parts of the track.

You can add a fade in effect, so the audio fades in at the beginning and fades out to silent at the end, using the 'fade duration' options.

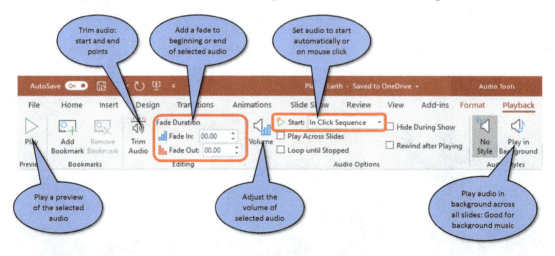

You can change whether you want the audio to play in one slide or across all your slides using 'play in background' option.

You can choose whether your audio plays automatically or if it starts when you click your mouse. You can adjust this using the 'start' setting on the audio options.

Screen Recording

Screen recording is useful if you are demonstrating something on your computer, or training someone to use a piece of software.

First, select a slide or insert a new one, then select your insert ribbon. From the insert ribbon click 'screen recording'.

You will need to select the area of your screen you want to record. To do this, click and drag the selection box across the part of your screen to record, eg, click the top corner and drag your mouse across the screen, as shown below.

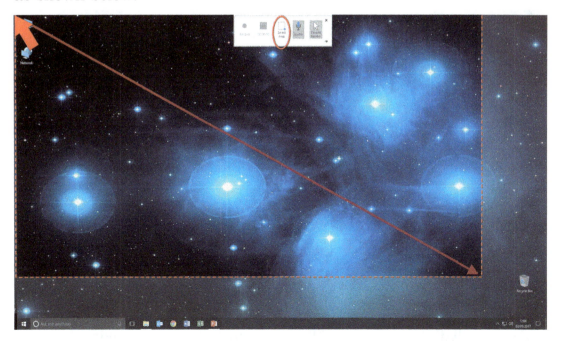

If you want the whole screen, click the top left corner and drag your mouse all the way to the bottom right corner.

When you have done that, click 'record' to start recording.

You'll get a 3 second countdown before you begin...

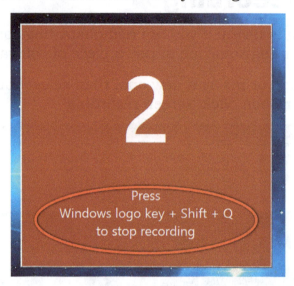

When the countdown hits zero, start the demonstration of what you're recording. PowerPoint will record your mouse clicks, applications opened and so on, within the area you selected in the previous step.

To stop recording, hold down Windows & Shift Key, then tap 'Q' - don't hold 'Q' down.

Your recorded screen video will appear in the selected slide. You may need to trim the screen recording because it's useful to remove the bits at the beginning where the control box is showing and at the end, so the screen recording just shows what you intended.

To do this, click on the screen recording video and from the playback ribbon click 'trim video'.

Now click and drag the beginning and end markers on the timeline to the points where you want the recording to start and where you want it to end.

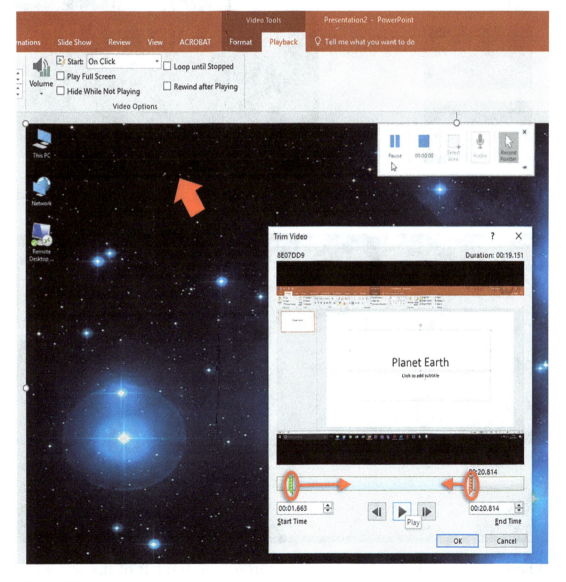

Click OK when you're done.

Recording Presentations

Record slide and animation timings, along with narrations, so the presentation will run through automatically.

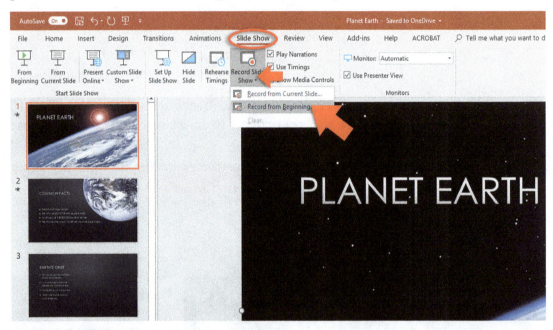

If you want to record narrations, click settings and make sure 'record audio' is checked and PowerPoint has found your microphone.

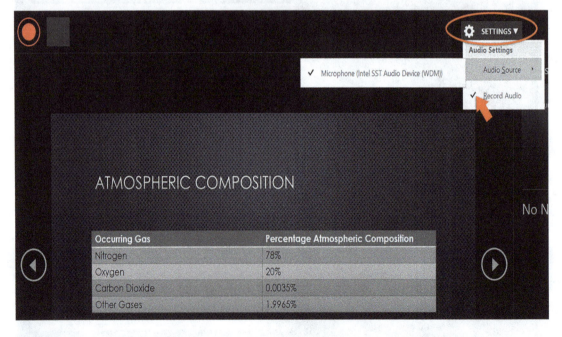

When you're ready, click the red button on the top left of the screen to start the recording.

Now give your presentation as if you were presenting to an audience, speaking into your microphone. It's best to be in a room where it is fairly quiet and with no echoes.

You can also use the screen annotation tools to draw on the slides, highlight points etc. PowerPoint will record your screen annotations, animations, bullets and transitions as you go through your presentation.

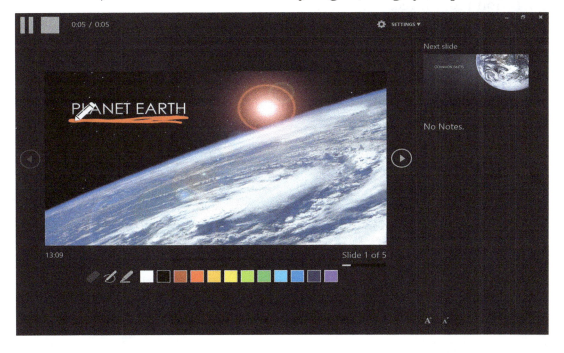

Once you are finished, click the stop button (large grey square on the top left).

Export your Presentation

You can export your presentation as a video file and upload it to YouTube or social media. This will include all your slide timings, transitions, animations, as well as your narrations.

Click File, then select export.

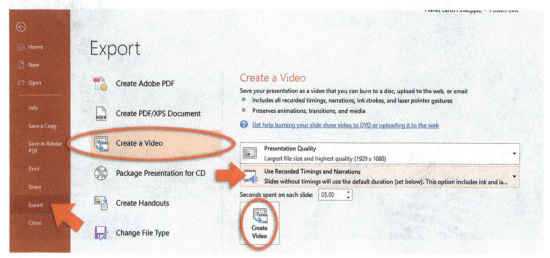

Set the presentation quality to the highest setting and select 'use recorded timings and narrations' to include your slide timings, annotations and narration recordings in the video.

Click 'create video', then select the folder you want to save it in. I'm saving my video in the 'videos' folder. Click 'save'.

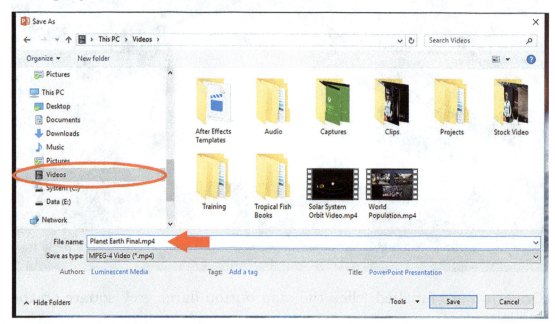

Photo Albums

There are two ways you can create photo albums. You can use the album generator on the insert ribbon, or you can use a photo album template from office.com.

First, lets have a look at some of the templates available on office.com. Go to FILE and click NEW.

Type 'Photo Album' into the search field. You'll see a list of templates appear in the search results.

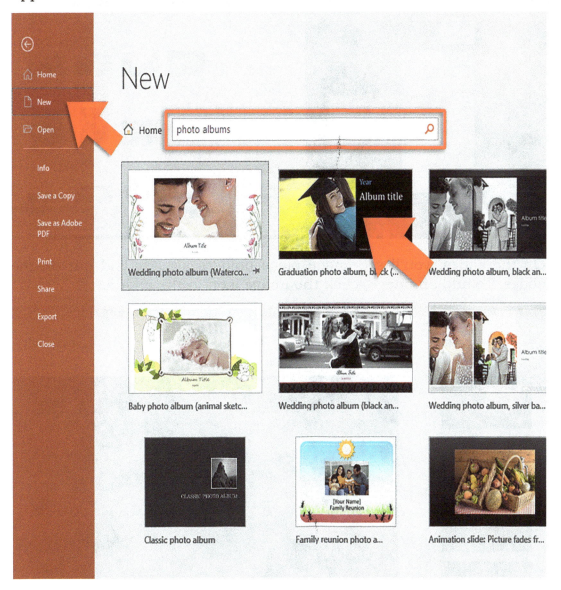

Double click on one of the template thumbnails to open a new presentation with that template.

Now you can start adding your images to the photo place holders in the presentation.

If there is a sample image already on the slide, to change it, right click and from the popup menu select 'change image'. From the slide out, select 'from file'. This is for photos stored on your computer.

On the slides, you'll see image place holders already laid out on the slides. To add an image, click the image icon in the middle.

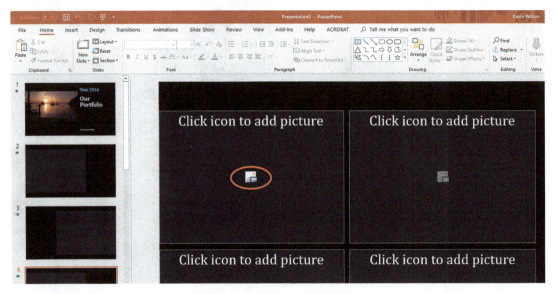

From the popup dialog box, select the image you want to insert. Do this with all the image place holders on all the slides.

You can also change the layouts of the photos. For example, on the second slide, say you wanted six small photos instead of one large photo.

To change the layout, click 'layout' from your home ribbon and select the layout from the drop down menu.

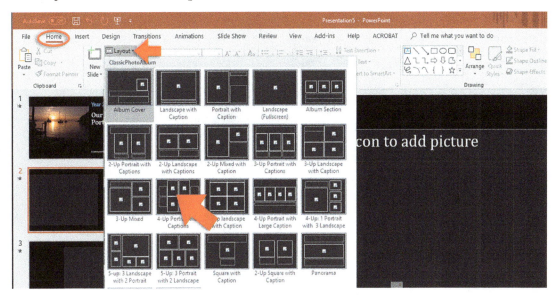

You can also add slide transitions as with ordinary slides, as well as animations for your photographs. To add animations, click your photo.

If you want to select more than one photo, hold down your control key while you select your photos.

From the animations ribbon, select an animation pre set. Do this with all the images you want effects on.

You can also create a photo album using the album generator on the insert ribbon.

Go to your insert ribbon, and select 'photo album'.

From the 'photo album' dialog box, click 'file/disk'.

Then from the 'insert new pictures' dialog box, navigate to your pictures folder, or where your photos are stored, and click to select the ones you want. If you are selecting more than one photo, hold down the control key while you select your photos.

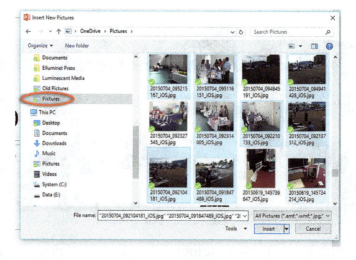

Click 'insert' when you're done.

You can also select a pre designed theme. To do this, click 'browse',

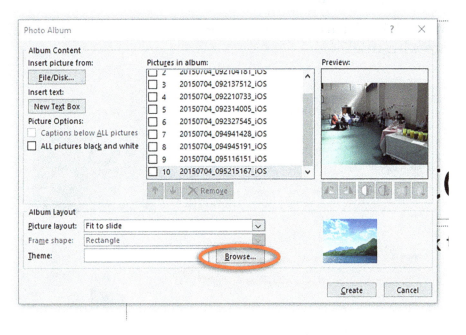

From the 'choose theme' dialog box, choose a theme from the list.

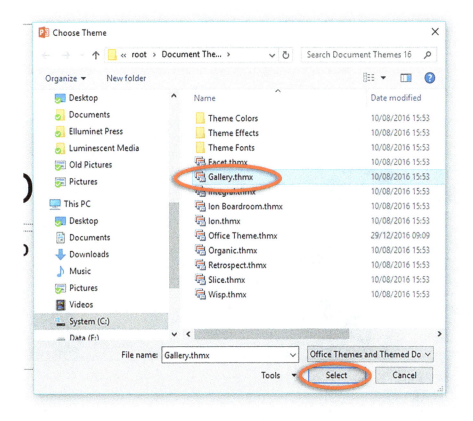

Click 'select' when you're done.

Chapter 7: Adding Multimedia

You can arrange the photos, one to a slide, more than one to a slide, or you can arrange to a slide with a title or caption.

To do this, click 'picture layout' and select an option. I'm going to select '1 picture with title'.

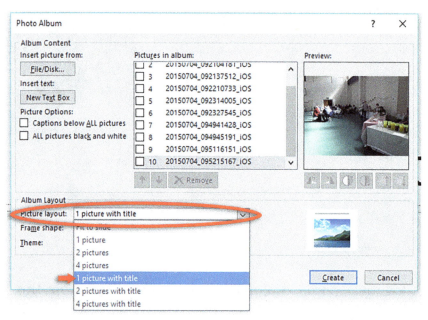

When you're done, click 'create'.

Now you can change the titles, add clipart and arrange the photos on your slides just like in any other PowerPoint presentation.

Edit your slides, add captions, headings and animations to your slides to make your album more exciting and interesting to watch.

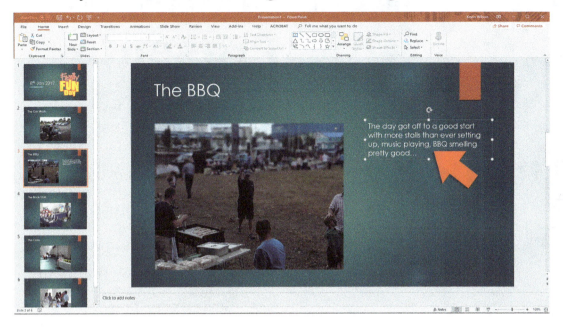

Run your photo album in the normal way. Press F5 on your keyboard.

Managing Presenta-tions

In this chapter, we'll explore how to save, open, print and export your presentation. We'll look at:

- Managing Presentations
- Opening a Saved Presentation
- Saving your Presentation
- Save as a Different Format
- Print your Slides

You'll need to download the source files from:

elluminetpress.com/ppt

Opening a Saved Presentation

If PowerPoint is already open you can open previously saved presentations by clicking the FILE menu on the top left of your screen.

From the orange bar on the left hand side click 'open', then click 'OneDrive - Personal'.

From the list, select the presentation you want to open. The presentation from the previous project was saved as 'planet earth.pptx', so this is the one I am going to open here.

For convenience, instead of searching through your OneDrive, PowerPoint lists all your most recently opened Presentations. You can view these by clicking 'Recent' instead of 'OneDrive - Personal'.

Your latest files will be listed first.

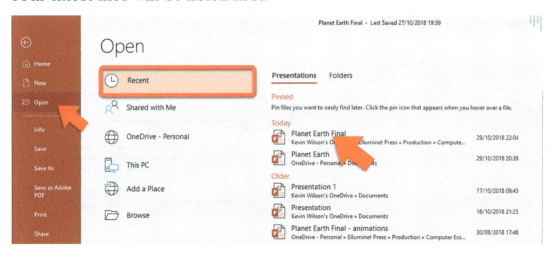

Double click the file name to open it.

Saving your Presentation

Click the small disk icon on the top left of the screen. If this is a new presentation that hasn't been saved before, PowerPoint will ask you where you want to save it. Save all your work onto your OneDrive.

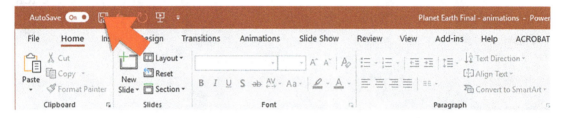

Click OneDrive Personal.

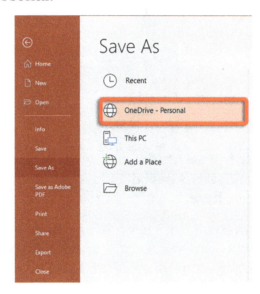

then enter a name for your presentation in the field indicated by the red arrow below.

When you have done that click save.

Save as a Different Format

To save your presentation in a different format, with your presentation open, click FILE.

From the backstage view, click 'Save As'.

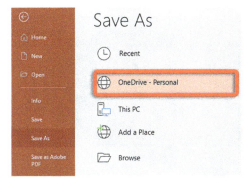

Select the folder you want to save your file in, eg, documents folder on your OneDrive.

Give your document a name, then underneath, click the down arrow and select a format. In this example, I am going to save the PowerPoint presentation as a PDF.

This is useful if you want to send a copy to someone that doesn't use Windows or have PowerPoint installed. Note with a PDF, you won't see all your animations or transitions in the file.

Click 'save' when you're done.

When you view the PDF version of your presentation, you'll see all the text and graphics.

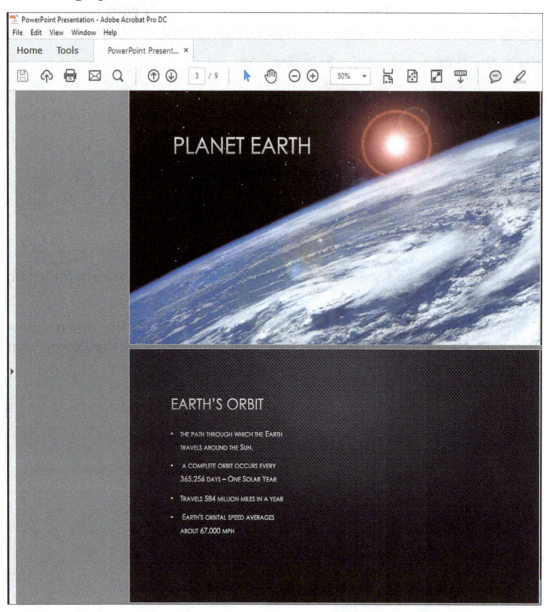

You can also save as a video. Use MPEG-4/MP4 video for Macs, Windows, Tablets, and Phones. Use Windows Media Video (WMV) if you're only using Windows based machines.

If you save your presentation as a video, you'll get all your transitions and animations saved along with any timings and voice recordings you have done. If you haven't, you'll get the default timings for each slide transition and animation. The video presentation will run automatically, you won't be able to click to advance any slides etc.

Print your Slides

To print your slides, click FILE on the top left hand corner of the screen, then select print.

In the screen below select the correct printer and number of copies you want.

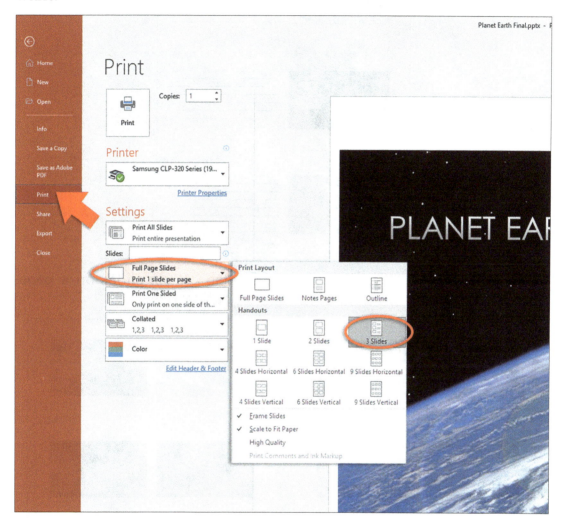

Then select how you want the slides to print out. Click where it says 'Full Page Slides'. 'Full Page Slides' prints out one slide per page and can be useful in some situations. If you are printing handouts, it makes sense to print more than one slide per page.

You'll see a pop up menu appear with some layout options for how to print out the slides on the page.

I usually select '3 slides', as it provides space for the audience to take notes on any particular slide.

You can then handout a copy of your slides to your audience so they can follow your presentation as you speak and take notes. I find this the most useful way to print slides.

If you just wanted the slides, you could also get six slides on a page. Just choose 'six horizontal slides' instead of '3 slides'.

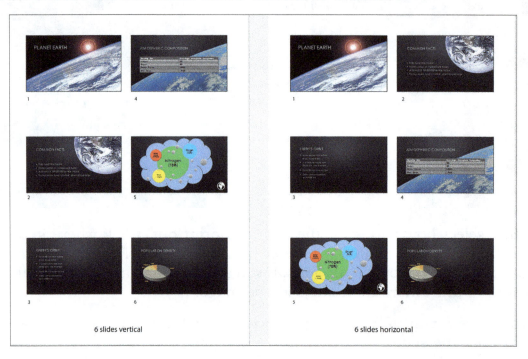

'Horizontal' means, the slides appear across the page rather than down the page. Notice how the slides are numbered above.

Sometimes it is useful to select 'black and white' or greyscale printing if you do not have a color printer.

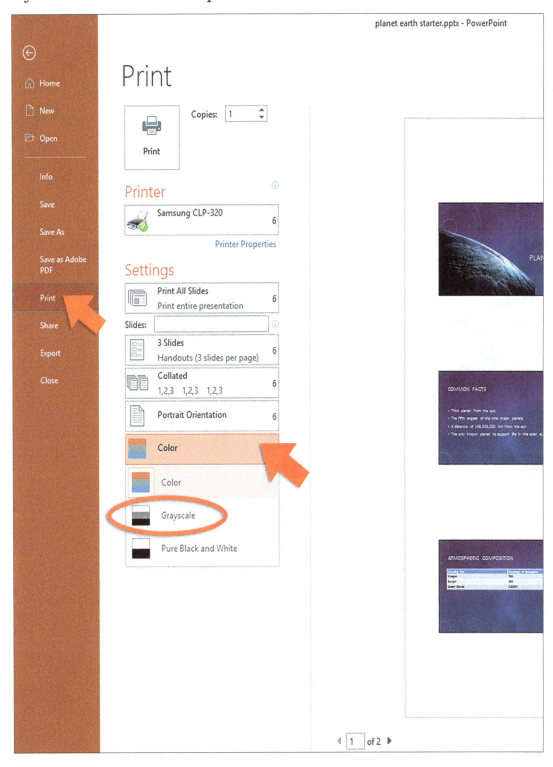

Click the print icon to print your presentation.

9

Sharing & Collabora-tion

In this chapter, we'll explore how to save, open, print and export your presentation. We'll look at:

- Sharing & Collaboration
- Introduction
- Collaborating in PowerPoint
- Managing Access

You'll need to download the source files from:

elluminetpress.com/ppt

Introduction

Microsoft Office applications such as Word, Excel, and PowerPoint allow You to save your files directly to OneDrive, making it easy to access files across all your devices.

On your PC/Mac, OneDrive creates a special folder that is synchronized with your OneDrive cloud storage. Any files or folders that you save to the OneDrive folder on your PC will automatically be uploaded to the cloud, and any changes made to files in the cloud will be copied back to the OneDrive folder on your PC. This is called synchronisation.

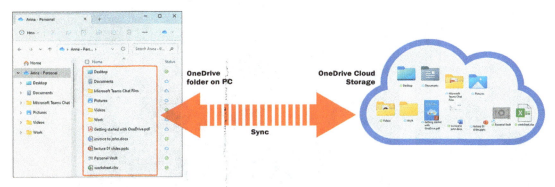

On mobile devices you can access all your OneDrive files without having to download them all to your device. This is called 'Files On-Demand'. This means all of your files and folders on OneDrive will be visible, but they are not be downloaded to your device until you actually need them. This feature saves space on your device and allows you to access your files from anywhere, even if you don't have enough storage on your local device.

Chapter 9: Sharing & Collaboration

OneDrive comes pre-installed on Windows 10/11 and you can access it through the File Explorer.

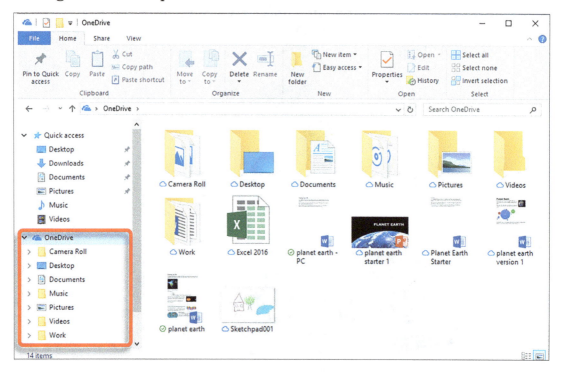

On a Mac, you can download the OneDrive app from the App Store. You'll find a OneDrive folder in the Finder app, and a shortcut to the OneDrive app along the top of the menu bar.

You can install the OneDrive app on mobile devices such as iPhones, iPads, and Android devices using the App Store.

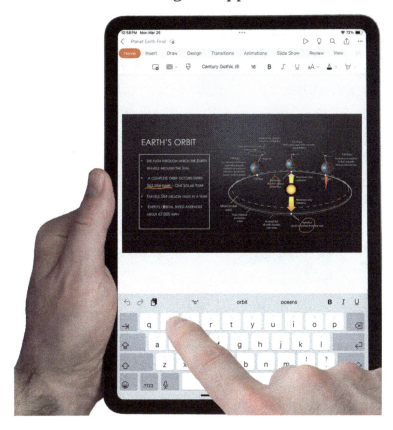

You can access OneDrive on the web using a web browser such as Chrome, Safari or Edge.

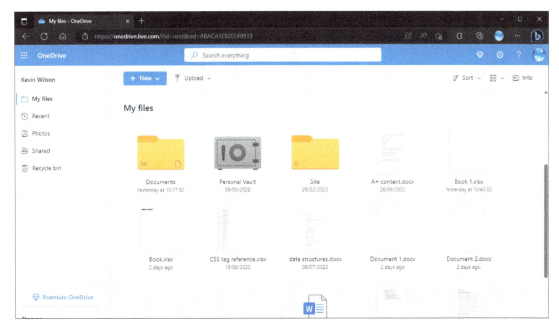

Collaborating in PowerPoint

Online collaboration in PowerPoint is designed to enhance team productivity by allowing multiple users to work on the same presentation simultaneously, regardless of their physical locations. Through real-time co-authoring, team members can see changes as they are made, identified by colored flags that show where others are editing.

Make sure your presentation is saved to OneDrive, then on the top right of PowerPoint's main screen, click the share button. You can share any document you are working on with friends and colleagues.

Enter the person's email address in the field at the top of the screen.

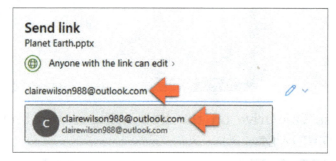

Now set the security permissions. Click the pencil icon on the right. Select 'can edit' to allow people to make changes to your presentation. If you don't want people to make changes, change this option to 'can view'.

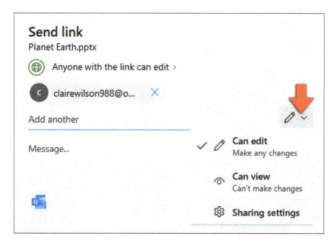

In the **Message** textbox add a personal message to the email that will be sent with the link.

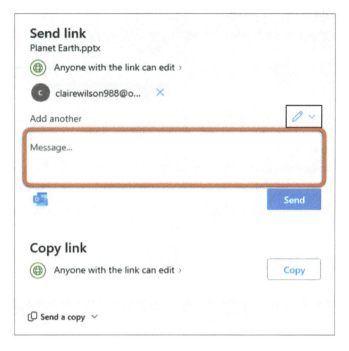

Set the remaining options if required.

Anyone with the link can edit at the top of the dialog box indicates the permission level that will be granted to the recipients. In this case, it's set to allow anyone with the link to edit the document. You could adjust this to view only if you don't want recipients to make changes.

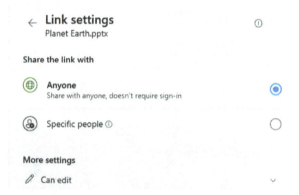

Copy link means instead of sending an email, you can generate a shareable link that you can distribute via another method, such as instant messaging or post on a website.

Send a copy allows you to send the actual presentation as an attachment to an email, rather than as a link to the cloud-stored presentation.

Click "Send", when you're done.

An email will be dispatched to the entered recipients with the link to the presentation, and if you've added a message, that will be included in the email.

When the other person checks their email, on the tablet in this demonstration, they will receive a message inviting them to open the presentation you just shared.

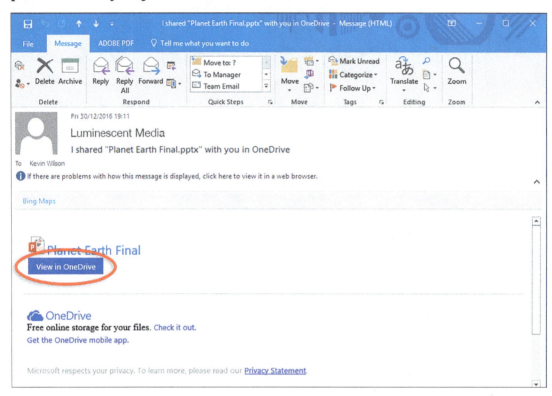

Click 'view in OneDrive', in the email message. The presentation will open in a web browser. Make sure you click 'sign in' on the top right of the screen and enter your Microsoft Account details when prompted.

Once you have signed in, click 'Edit Presentation', then click 'edit in PowerPoint'

This will download the document and open it up in PowerPoint installed on your computer (the tablet in this demo).

Here, the user on the tablet can start editing the presentation. As an example, they're going to add a bullet point to the list.

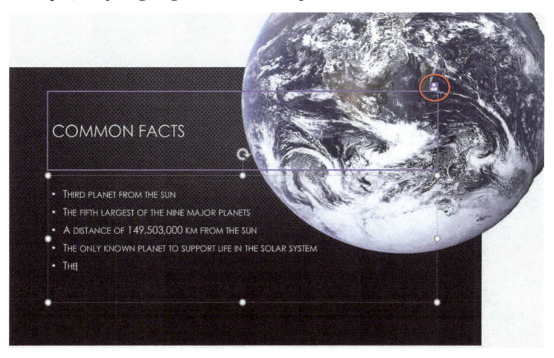

You'll be able to see who is editing what, indicated with a user icon on the top right of the text boxes, circled below.

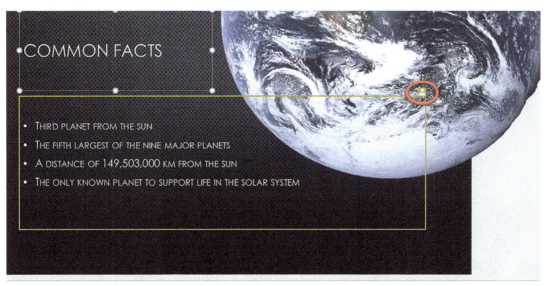

We can see here on the laptop screen, that the user on the tablet is editing the bottom text box.

Managing Access

To manage access to a shared PowerPoint file, select the file in OneDrive or SharePoint, then click 'share' in the upper-right corner of the screen. Select 'Manage access'.

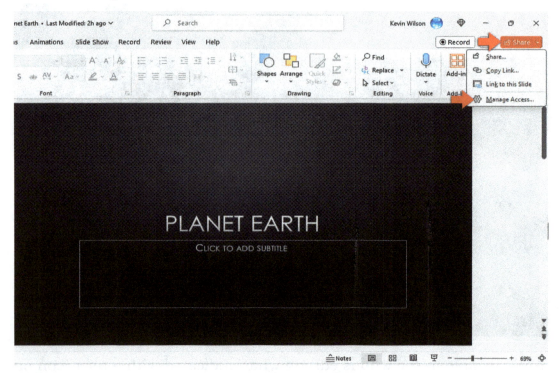

You can stop sharing the file entirely, delete specific sharing links, or change permissions for individuals who have direct access. Click on the user you want to manage.

Under 'ways this person has access', click on 'direct access'.

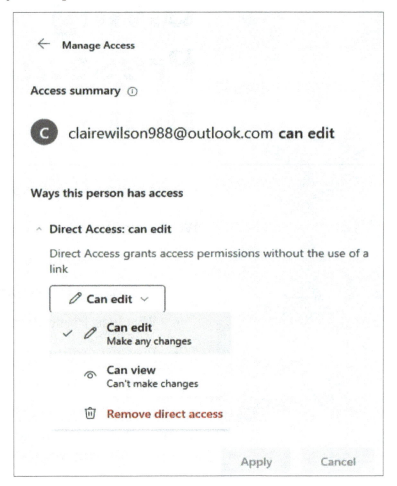

From the "Ways this person has access" section, you can see that you have the option to change their permission level. If you want to change their ability to edit the file, you can choose "Can view" to downgrade their access or select "Remove direct access" to revoke their access entirely. These settings are crucial for managing who can see and edit your shared files.

10

Giving Presenta- tions

In this chapter, we'll explore how to set up and give your presentation. We'll look at:

- Giving Presentations

- Setting Up Projectors

- Wireless Presenting

- Present Online

- Audience Engagement

To help you better understand this section, take a look at the video resources. Open your web browser and navigate to the following website:

elluminetpress.com/ppt-pres

You'll also need to download the source files from:

elluminetpress.com/ppt

Setting Up Projectors

Connect your laptop to your projector. Modern projectors either use a VGA or an HDMI cable to connect. The projector in the example uses a VGA, but the principle is the same regardless of what cable you're using.

Connect the other end to your laptop

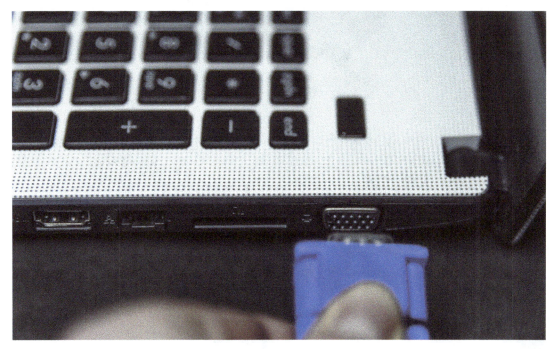

DVI

Digital Video Interface is a video display interface used to connect a video source (eg your computer) to a display device, such as an HD ready TV, computer monitor or projector.

HDMI

High Definition Media Interface, is a combined audio/video interface for carrying video and audio data from a High Definition device such as a games console or computer to a high end computer monitor, video projector, or High Definition digital television.

Pictured below is Standard HDMI & Micro HDMI.

VGA

Video Graphics Array is a 15-pin connector found on many computers and laptops and is used to connect to projectors, computer monitors and LCD television sets.

Plug the power lead into the projector.

Now fire up the projector. Once the projector is running, start up your laptop.

On your laptop, the best way to use PowerPoint is to use an extended screen display. This means that the projector screen is an extension of your laptop screen, rather than a duplicate. This will allow you to have notes and to see the next slides coming up in your presentation - the presenter display.

In Windows 10, to do this, hold down the windows key then tap 'P'. From the side panel that opens up, click 'extend'.

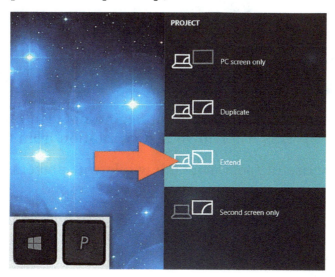

Running your Presentation

The controls for running your presentation can be found on the slide show ribbon.

On the right hand side of the ribbon, click the drop down box next to 'monitor' and select the name of your second screen or projector.

This tells PowerPoint, which screen to display your presentation on for your audience to see. Your laptop or tablet screen is your presenter view. This will show you any notes you have written as well as the next slide. If you want this feature, tick 'use presenter view'.

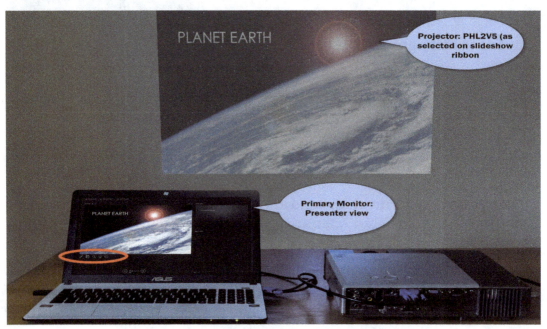

To run your presentation, click 'from beginning' icon on the left hand side (or press F5). This will run your presentation from the first slide.

You have a few useful tools available while you present (circled in the image above).

You can zoom into a specific part of the slide to highlight it, by clicking the magnifying glass icon and positioning the rectangle over the part of the slide you want to show.

You can annotate your slides with notes to help your audience understand your point. Click the pen tool, select the pen and draw on the slide with your finger, a stylus or a mouse.

You can also present with a Windows 10 tablet running PowerPoint connected to a projector.

You may need a mini display port to VGA adapter, or a USB3 to VGA adapter to connect directly to the projector.

Wireless Presenting

If you're using Windows 10, there is a feature that allows you to project to another Windows 10 device. So you could have your Windows 10 laptop hooked up to the projector and use your Windows 10 tablet to wirelessly project to your laptop.

Both your laptop and tablet will need to be on the same wireless network for this to work. Some laptops wont support this, but most modern ones do. To connect, on your tablet open your action centre and tap 'connect'.

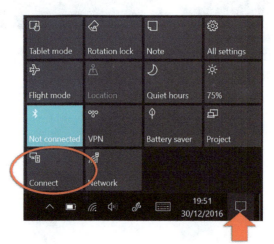

Your Windows 10 tablet will scan the network for your laptop... In this demo, the laptop's network name is 'Asus-Laptop' and the tablet's name is 'surfaceone'.

Once found, you'll see your laptop appear in the search results. Double tap on the name to connect.

On your laptop click 'yes' on the connection prompt that will appear on the bottom right of your screen.

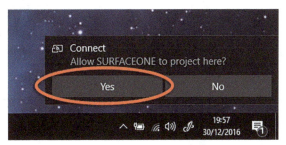

Once you click 'yes', you'll see a blue screen on your laptop while your devices connect.

If you're having trouble, make sure your laptop is set up to receive. Go to your settings icon on the start menu, click system, then click 'projecting to this PC'.

Make sure your laptop supports wireless projection, and that the settings are set up as shown in the screen above. Also check your wifi settings on your laptop and tablet.

Now you can start PowerPoint on your tablet and you'll see the screen project to the laptop.

With the laptop connected to your projector, you're all set to present with a wireless tablet.

You can remote control the laptop from your surface tablet and present wirelessly, using the ink features of PowerPoint to highlight important points and concepts you want your audience to take note of.

You can now use PowerPoint on your tablet and run your presentation.

You can use the touch features on your tablet, such as a stylus and annotate your slides as you present.

Present Online

You can set up a presentation and present it online, so anyone with a link to your presentation can 'tune in' and watch.

To do this, open your presentation and from the slideshow ribbon, click 'present online'.

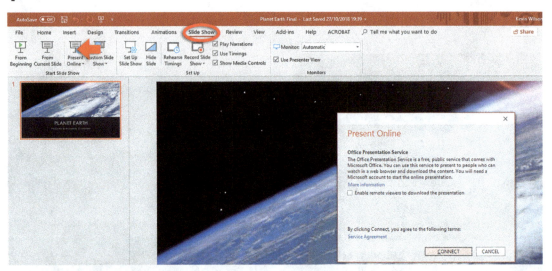

From the dialog box that appears, click 'connect'. *If you want your audience to be able to download a copy of your PowerPoint presentation, click the 'enable remove viewers to download the presentation'.*

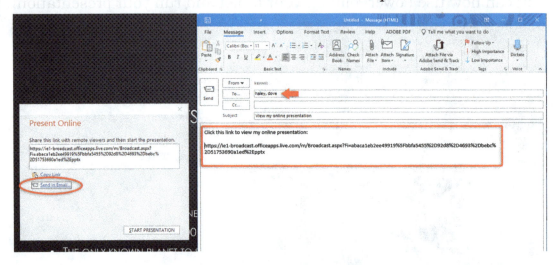

Next, invite the people you want to see your presentation. If you have Outlook installed on your machine, click 'send an email'. Add the email addresses to the email message that pops up. You can also click 'copy link' to copy to your clipboard and paste into sms/text message, imessage or skype.

When you are ready to begin, click 'start presentation' to begin your broadcast.

In the demonstration below, the laptop on the left is hosting the presentation.

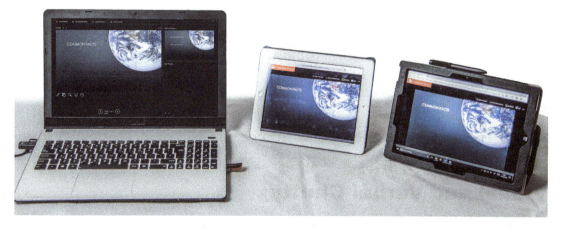

The iPad and the Surface Tab are viewing the presentation in a web browser. These could be anywhere with an internet connection.

Audience Engagement

Delivering a presentation is not just about conveying information; it's about captivating your audience, ensuring they understand your message, and leaving a lasting impression. Effective delivery and audience engagement play crucial roles in achieving these objectives. Here are key strategies to enhance your presentation delivery and engage your audience.

Confidence and Presence

Confidence is contagious. Stand tall, maintain eye contact, and speak with conviction.

Project your voice clearly and vary your tone to keep your audience engaged.

Embrace pauses strategically to emphasize important points and allow time for reflection.

Know Your Material

Thoroughly familiarize yourself with your presentation content. Confidence stems from competence.

Anticipate potential questions or objections and prepare thoughtful responses.

Avoid reading directly from slides or notes. Instead, speak conversationally and refer to visuals as aids, not scripts.

Connect with Your Audience

Establish rapport by acknowledging your audience's interests, concerns, or experiences related to your topic.

Use inclusive language and address individuals directly, fostering a sense of involvement.

Incorporate relatable anecdotes, humor, or personal stories to forge emotional connections.

Visual and Verbal Clarity

Ensure your slides are visually appealing, concise, and easy to read from a distance.

Use visuals sparingly to complement your spoken words rather than compete with them.

Articulate your points clearly, avoiding jargon or overly technical language that may alienate some audience members.

Engage Through Interaction

Encourage active participation through questions, polls, or interactive exercises.

Incorporate multimedia elements such as videos, live demonstrations, or interactive simulations to enhance engagement.

Foster a collaborative atmosphere where audience members feel valued and involved in the learning process.

Storytelling and Emotion

Craft narratives that evoke emotion and resonate with your audience's experiences and aspirations.

Use storytelling techniques to illustrate key concepts, humanize data, and make abstract ideas tangible.

Appeal to both logic and emotion, balancing facts with storytelling to create a compelling narrative arc.

Adaptability and Flexibility

Remain adaptable to unforeseen circumstances, such as technical glitches or unexpected audience reactions.

Be prepared to adjust your pacing, content, or delivery style based on audience feedback and engagement levels.

Embrace spontaneity and welcome opportunities for organic interaction and dialogue

Feedback and Continuous Improvement

Seek feedback from trusted peers, mentors, or audience members to identify areas for improvement.

Reflect on each presentation experience and identify lessons learned to refine your delivery techniques.

Resources

To help you understand the procedures and concepts explored in this book, we have developed some video resources and app demos for you to use, as you work through the book.

To find the resources, open your web browser and navigate to the following website

elluminetpress.com/ppt

At the beginning of each chapter, you'll find a website that contains the resources for that chapter.

File Resources

To save the files into your OneDrive documents folder, right click on the icons above and select 'save target as' (or 'save link as', on some browsers). In the dialog box that appears, select 'OneDrive', click the 'Documents' folder, then click 'save'.

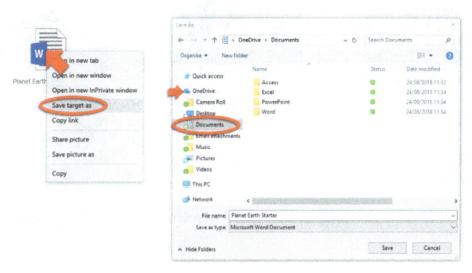

The sample images are stored in a compressed zip file. To download the zip file, right click on the zip icon on the page above, 'Sample Images. zip. Select 'save target as' (or 'save link as', on some browsers) and save it into 'pictures' on your OneDrive folder.

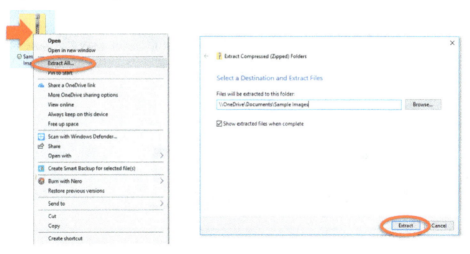

Once you have downloaded the zip file, go to your 'pictures' folder in your OneDrive, right click on the zip file, and select 'extract all' from the menu. From the dialog box that appears click 'extract'. This will create a new folder in your pictures called 'sample images'. You'll find the images used in the examples in the books.

Video Resources

The video resources are grouped into sections for each chapter in the book. Click the thumbnail link to open the section.

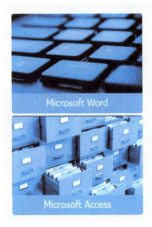

When you open the link to the video resources, you'll see a thumbnail list at the bottom.

Click on the thumbnail for the particular video you want to watch. Most videos are between 30 and 60 seconds outlining the procedure, others are a bit longer.

When the video is playing, hover your mouse over the video and you'll see some controls...

Let's take a look at the video controls. On the left hand side:

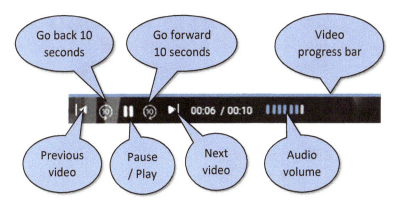

On the right hand side:

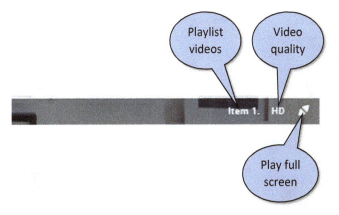

Scanning the Codes

At the beginning of each chapter, you'll a QR code you can scan with your phone to access additional resources, files and videos.

iPhone

To scan the code with your iPhone/iPad, open the camera app.

Frame the code in the middle of the screen. Tap on the website popup at the top.

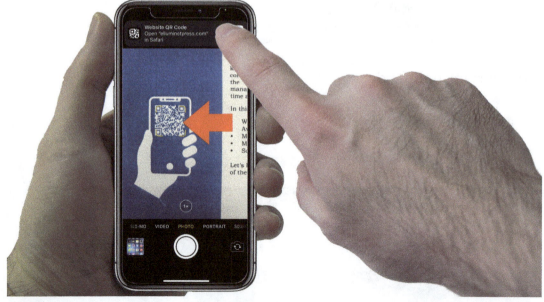

Android

To scan the code with your phone or tablet, open the camera app.

Frame the code in the middle of the screen. Tap on the website popup at the top.

If it doesn't scan, turn on 'Scan QR codes'. To do this, tap the settings icon on the top left. Turn on 'scan QR codes'.

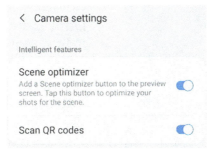

If the setting isn't there, you'll need to download a QR Code scanner. Open the Google Play Store, then search for "QR Code Scanner".

Index

Index

W

SOMETHING
NOT COVERED?

We want to create the best possible resources to help you learn and get things done, so if we've missed anything out, then please get in touch using the links below and let us know. Thanks.

 office@elluminetpress.com

 elluminetpress.com/feedback

www.ingramcontent.com/pod-product-compliance
Lightning Source LLC
Chambersburg PA
CBHW060130060326

40690CB00018B/3821